THE
HOUSEPLANT
SURVIVAL GUIDE

THE
HOUSEPLANT
SURVIVAL GUIDE

PAT REGEL

The Taunton Press

Front cover photographer: Scott Phillips
Photos by Scott Phillips were shot at Lexington Gardens, Newtown, CT

Taunton
BOOKS & VIDEOS

for fellow enthusiasts

First printing: March 1997
Printed in the United States of America

The Taunton Press, 63 South Main Street,
PO Box 5506, Newtown, CT 06470-5506

Created for The Taunton Press by
Storey Communications, Inc., Schoolhouse Road,
Pownal, VT 05261

Library of Congress Cataloging-in-Publication Data

Regel, Pat, 1947–
      The houseplant survival guide / Pat Regel.
            p.   cm.
      Includes index.
      ISBN 1-56158-186-0 (alk. paper)
      1. House plants.   2. Indoor gardening.   I. Title.
SB419.R43   1997   96-29564
635.9'65—dc21   CIP

For my husband, Terry, who took time out in the writing of his own books to assist me with mine.

CONTENTS

INTRODUCTION

My enjoyment of houseplants goes way back to my college days. I can remember when a pot of pothos was considered sophisticated—and about the only green and living thing you could find in the way of houseplants.

I remember the absolute craze for houseplants that blossomed in the 1960s. Everyone had them. Everyone was talking about them. Magazines and books on houseplant care appeared almost overnight. Fledgling radio talk shows dedicated to gardening spent portions of each show discussing mealy bug infestations, and houseplant clubs began taking root and growing throughout the country.

It was something everyone got into. Homeowners and apartment dwellers alike tended pots and transplanted their way through the 1970s and into the early 1980s.

But, as is the case with all fads, the craze wound down.

Now, in the late nineties, there are rumblings of a resurgence. Things are slowly coming full circle. Houseplants are making a strong comeback as people spend more time entertaining themselves at home.

The place where you used to go to hang your hat and change your clothes now has everything you used to leave the house for—from movies to exercise equipment. With today's technology, you can even log in a full day's work without walking out the front door. It's not "Don't leave home without it"; it's "Why leave home at all?"

Enjoying familiar surroundings with family and friends and getting away from the daily office grind has become fashionable. Home gardening interest has skyrocketed, and my guess is that homeowner and apartment dweller alike will be preparing yet another assault on the houseplant stalls before long, looking for something exciting.

Plants are being used more now than ever for decorating and creating lush interiors. In fact, this appears to be the sole purpose of some companies—to accessorize rooms by using only plants. These people know that houseplants can remove the hard edges from cold, bulky, office furniture and soften the "hardscape" of a room's interior while creating interest. The outside can be brought inside in a most pleasing way.

And plants can add color and fragrance, too. Some plants are variegated; others produce eye-catching blooms that work well with a room's decor. Plants also refresh the air, which often becomes stale quickly in rooms left unaired during the winter months. The sweet, clean fragrance of chlorophyll from the leaves of a large basket of Swedish ivy will "perfume" a room. I keep a basketful near the kitchen to freshen the room of cooking odors.

But there are still some people who wonder if you really get your money's worth when you buy a houseplant. Well, consider this for a moment: A $10 bottle of wine for your meal this evening will last you for the duration of the evening. But a $10 houseplant will give you years of enjoyment and (if cared for properly) will provide you with many other similar houseplants when it comes time to divide the overgrown mother plant.

I knew a couple some 20 years ago who lived in an apartment and used to leave home each Saturday morning and go to a favorite garden center.

They never bought anything.

When I asked them why they went, they confessed that they just "wanted to be among green things." They said they never considered buying plants because a few unsuccessful tries had proved to be discouraging.

"I guess we just have 'brown thumbs,'" she said. "We'd rather sit in our own home Saturday mornings, sipping coffee among the plants, but it's not possible. So, we go where the plants are."

Listen, folks. There's no such thing as a "brown thumb." There are, however, people who don't know what houseplants require in the way of light, water, and a few other things. But once plant requirements are understood and provided for, anyone can grow them. No special talents are required.

Are you going to lose a few plants in the early stages as you learn? Yes. It's unavoidable and part of the learning process. The plant would normally do just fine in its own environment. But, since it's stuck in a pot and its roots can't go after what the plant needs, it depends on you to provide the necessities. Learn these necessities, and you can grow the plant.

It's that simple.

In this book, I'll discuss what it takes to give your plants the things they need to flourish in your home for years to come. I'll also try to anticipate the questions you would ask if we were talking about plants over cups of coffee. With this approach, my goal is to make the book more user friendly and personal.

"Returnees" take heart. Everything you learned about houseplants years ago will come back to you. Your backlog of stored knowledge won't have been wasted. You'll find a refresher course within these pages as well as some new ideas for houseplant care and enjoyment.

Those of you new to the satisfying hobby of growing houseplants have missed the first generation of houseplant gardeners: the First Wave, so to speak. You'll need some of the basics to get you started and prepare you for the Second Wave, which is predicted for the rest of this century and into the next.

This book has been written for you both (beginners and returnees) in the hope that your skill will advance as well as your love for houseplant gardening.

May all of your fingers be green.

CHAPTER ONE LIGHT

I s there such a thing as a "brown thumb" gardener? My answer is always no. Gardeners don't have brown thumbs; they have a lack of information. And there's nothing better at killing plants than a lack of information on how to care for them.

You will learn about plants by owning and caring for them. There is no other way. Does this mean you'll kill a few until you get the hang of it? Yes. And after you've killed a few, you'll have learned not to kill more. You must acquire plant knowledge firsthand. Experience is everything—nothing can replace it.

People who know plants know plant requirements and how to satisfy them. And that is the difference between a green thumb and a brown thumb gardener. It also leads us into this all-important chapter.

Before we explore the indoor green world of houseplant gardening and discuss this rewarding hobby, we need to do a bit of study—let's make a few culture notes.

First, what do I mean by culture? I'm talking about the basic requirements that plants need to survive, grow, and prosper.

The culture of a plant is always static; it never changes. Your own personal "culture" and environmental needs, however, can be altered—they aren't static—because we can adjust to just about any environment, including outer space, and we can move about—we aren't confined to pots. Now, you also can take your plant anywhere you want, but its specific cultural needs will always be the same. This means that you must alter the surrounding conditions so that the plant's environmental and cultural needs can be met. Once this is done, you can grow the plant anywhere. That's why orchids can be grown under artificial lights aboard a submarine that remains at sea for six months out of the year.

Here are the basic cultural requirements of plants, which we'll talk about throughout the next six chapters. Become

Many different plants, such as this ivy, can produce luscious growth without the benefit of a sunny window.

familiar with these requirements, and your brown thumb will disappear.

- Light
- Water
- Temperature
- Soil
- Humidity
- Ventilation
- Food

After working with plants for a while, you'll see that each plant has its own culture, but it has something more. It has its own idiosyncrasies—its own likes and dislikes, its own peculiarities (just as people have)—which set it apart from other plants. I think it's the mastering of these idiosyncrasies that adds to the green thumb's success with plants.

Why Light Is Essential

Let's start with the most important ingredient: light.

Without it, plants can't live. Within a matter of days, the leaves of some light-sensitive plants turn yellow. Then they begin the long spiral downward in a lingering, unattractive state until they finally die. They hold on until the bitter end—waiting for light that never comes. I remember a peculiar conversation I once had with someone who "knew" plants. She had bought a corn plant (sometimes called corn palm, *Dracaena fragrans* 'Massangeana'). I noticed that it stood in a dark, sunless corner and wondered if she moved it into the light each day. She said no, this plant is so easy to grow in the home because it doesn't require any light at all. On my next visit to the house, a month later, the plant was missing from its usual dark recess. It had been thrown out a few days before. The

plantless woman declared that she'd never been able to grow anything because of her brown thumb.

Plants are different from animals. We must get our food from several sources, but plants can make their own food. Light is important to plants because they use it to produce their food. They are able to take light and photosynthesize it into sugars that will be used for cell growth and repair.

If a plant can't get light for extended periods of time, problems begin. It will stop growing and begin to use up its stored food. This is what a bulb does beneath the soil. It uses its stored food to give it energy to sprout and push upward through the soil until the sunlight can take over and help it photosynthesize the sugars it needs for food.

Have you ever kept bulbs in the garage for a long period of time, knowing full well that they needed to be planted? We've all done this. Come back a few months later, and they're all shriveled—the stored food had been consumed.

This is one of the reasons why the aftereffects of nuclear warfare would be so disastrous. In my younger years when the threat of nuclear war was only too real, scientists gave the survivors of an attack (if there were any) some cheery, uplifting news: The planet would be so enveloped in nuclear cloud cover that plants would be unable to gather sunlight that provides the energy for photosynthesis to occur. In short, there would be no sunlight, plants couldn't make their food, and they would die.

These were not words to gladden the heart.

Today, we hear of studies being done that point out the importance of sunlight to humans. It seems that depression in humans may be linked to lack of

How can I tell if my plants aren't getting enough light?

Here are some things to look for:

- Leaves are smaller than normal
- Leaves are pale in color
- No growth from the growing tip of the plant
- Growth is spindly with long spaces between leaves
- Lower leaves turn yellow and fall off
- Bloom is poor, if any at all
- Variegated leaves turn green

Houseplants are often displayed all together in the garden center, but each has its own light requirements. Flowering plants require the most light, followed by variegated foliage plants. Foliage plants, at left, need the least amount of light.

For cacti and succulents, be generous with sun but miserly with water.

sunlight. The overcast, gray, sunless winter months do appear to give rise to depression in sensitive people, but those few early bright days at the end of winter give everyone relief. The popularity of sunrooms (Florida rooms in some quarters) and plant rooms attest to our love of and need for sunshine.

Amount of Light

When you determine a plant's light requirements, also consider the amount of light, which means how long the plant is actually in the light.

Do your plants get four hours of sunlight each day while sitting on a windowsill, or do they get eight hours? If the plant needs direct sun conditions, you can bet that the more light it gets, the more robust growth it exhibits. There are, however, some plants that don't require long hours of light, and may even be harmed by it.

Here are some rules of thumb regarding light:

- Foliage plants need bright light, no direct sunlight.
- Variegated foliage plants need more light than do nonvariegated plants.
- Flowering plants need some direct sunlight.
- Cacti and succulents need some direct sunlight.

Intensity of Light

The intensity of light is different from the amount of light. If you walk from a sunny window toward the center of the room, you'll pass through all of the exposures of light suitable for growing plants. You will have traveled from full sun to shade in 8 ft. to 10 ft.

A simple discussion of light exposures will help you plan where to put what plant. Also, remember when you buy plants to look for the "plant tags" (also called "culture tags"). They should come with your plant and tell you what light requirement is needed. Become familiar with your plant tags. In time, you'll know the cultural information on them but you should keep them on hand for future reference.

Sometimes the plant tags tell you to put the plant in a south or west window in the winter and a north or east window in the summer. The reason for this has to do with the light intensity.

Sunlight is more intense in the summer. This means that it's more likely to burn a plant because the rays are stronger than they are in the winter. So a plant

Plant tags provide essential plant care information, so be sure to save them for future reference.

INTENSITY OF LIGHT ON PLANTS	
Light Exposure	Plants
Full sun (direct sunlight): within 2 ft. of a south-facing window; intense light; some flowering plants can grow here	Amaryllis, bougainvillea, cacti, chrysanthemum, citrus, coleus, forced spring-flowering bulbs, geraniums, hibiscus, jasmine, lantana, most herbs, oxalis, outdoor annuals, roses, succulents
Some direct sun: within 2 ft. to 2½ ft. of an east- or west-facing window; some flowering plants can grow here	Asparagus fern, *Capsicum*, chrysanthemum, *Cordyline*, ficus, *Gynura*, *Hoya*, impatiens, *Plumbago*, poinsettia, *Sansevieria*
Bright, sunless (indirect sunlight): within a 5-ft. area around a window—no direct sun; some flowering plants can grow here	African violets, asparagus fern, azalea, bromeliads, *Chlorophytum*, *Clivia*, columnea, cyclamen, dieffenbachia, *Monstera*, peperomia, philodendron, *Pilea*, pothos, *Schefflera*, *Spathiphyllum*, zygocactus
Semishade: within 5 ft. to 8 ft. of a sunless window; few flowering plants can grow here	*Aglaonema, Aspidistra,* dracaena, fatsia, ferns, fittonia, ivy, *Maranta*, philodendron, *Sansevieria, Tolmiea*
Shade: poorly lit area away from window; enough light to read by; no flowering plants can grow here	*Aglaonema, Aspidistra, Asplenium,* ivy, fittonia, pothos, *Sansevieria*

Do white walls affect the intensity of light?

Yes. You even can improve the reflected light with white or cream-colored walls.

How do I know how much light my houseplant needs?

When purchasing a houseplant, always look for the plant tag (also called a culture tag). You'll see it either in the pot or attached to the plant. Many of the requirements needed to grow the plant will be listed on the tag. It's a good idea to keep the tag attached to the pot until you become acquainted with the information printed on it.

Plant tags are a good way to learn about each plant's individual requirements—collect them, and you'll become knowledgeable about many houseplants.

Light exposures from a south-facing window

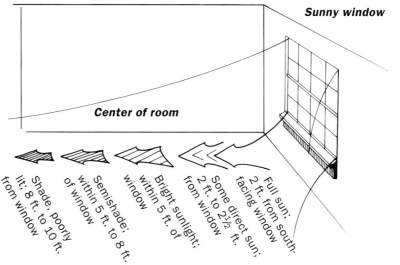

Sunny window

Center of room

Shade: poorly lit: 8 ft. to 10 ft. from window

Semishade: within 5 ft. to 8 ft. of window

Bright sunlight; within 5 ft. of window

Some direct sun; 2 ft. to 2½ ft. from window

Full sun; 2 ft. from south-facing window

Light levels drop dramatically as you move away from a window. Don't place plants with high light requirements too far away from windows.

Light exposures from all directions

North
Semishade: within 5 ft. to 8 ft. of a sunless window
Shade: poorly lit area away from window

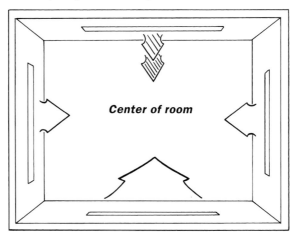

West
Some direct sun: within 2 ft. to 2½ ft. Stronger sun in the afternoon

Center of room

East
Some direct sun: within 2 ft. to 2½ ft. Stronger sun in the morning

South
Full sun: within 2 ft. of window
Bright, indirect sun: within 5 ft. of window

Choose a window for your plants carefully. In the Northern Hemisphere, the sun's travel across the sky brings more rays to southern windows than to any others.

sitting in a south-facing window in the summer may get leaf burn unless the plant requires this much intense light. But even longtime houseplant growers who know their plants well can make mistakes. Taking a plant from a north-facing window in winter and setting it in a south-facing window in summer could result in burn damage to tender leaves—they may look as if they'd been scorched.

Plants need time to adjust to light levels and light intensity. They must be introduced to new light conditions gradually.

Turning your pots

To turn a pot means that a potted plant is rotated one-quarter of the way around every few weeks.

Turning your pots does something important for plant growth. Turning guarantees even growth on all sides of a plant. If pots aren't turned regularly, the plant will lean toward the light, and the side of the plant that is away from the sunlight will become unattractively elongated. Soon, the plant begins to look misshapen, leggy, or spindly. What you want is tight foliage—full, compact, close growth. This comes only when plants receive their individual optimum light requirements.

After the pot has been turned, the part of the plant that was farthest away from the sun is now closer. This means that the rays of the sun will be much more intense on tender leaves than when they were turned away from the sun.

Exceptions: Even if you're not moving your plants closer to the light, you can still burn tender leaves simply by turning your pots. Don't turn a pot if the plant is in bud or about to bloom. Let it finish its bloom cycle first—then you can turn it.

This scented geranium was not turned, so it's craning its leaves toward sunlight. Note the leggy growth, a sign of inadequate light.

Plants are finicky at bloom time, and they may resent being moved. Some "voice" their opposition by refusing to bloom. During times like this, I'm at my wit's end—being put in my place by vegetation!

But a plant doesn't have to be in flower in order to resent being moved. Weeping fig (*Ficus benjamina*) is famous for being disagreeable when moved. It can voice its displeasure by promptly turning yellow and dropping all of its leaves. Great.

Wash your windows

There's something about glass windows that people don't realize: If clean, the windows will magnify sunlight, and plants sitting close to them will receive the full force of the sun's rays.

Washing windows both inside and out will guarantee several months of bright winter growing light. It may not surprise you that dirty windows can cut light intensity in half, even if plants are close to the panes.

What happens if houseplants get too much light?

Here are some things to look for:

- Leaves may burn—look for scorched patches
- Leaves may wilt at noon
- Leaves look washed out and dull
- Leaves may completely "burn up" (become dry and fall off)

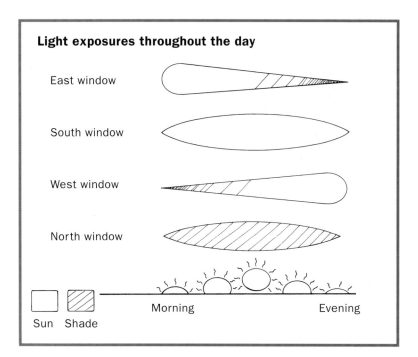

Light exposures throughout the day

East window

South window

West window

North window

☐ ▨
Sun Shade

Morning   Evening

Artificial Light

If you don't have much light in your apartment or home, have you thought of growing houseplants under artificial light? Growers, of course, have been doing this for some time, but many people haven't tried it. Here's how artificial light works. All wavelengths of light are needed for plant growth, but blue and red, which control photosynthesis and plant growth, are used most. Outdoors, plants use the blue part of the light spectrum for leaf growth, but prefer the red for developing flowers. Fluorescent tubes are able to imitate the light of the natural spectrum and give off blue and red light just as the sun does.

An artificial light setup calls for a series of two or four fluorescent tubes mounted underneath a reflector. The reflector-tube setup is then installed over the growing area so that the light is directed down onto the plants. And that's really all there is to it.

If you use artificial lights, though, water from the plants is absorbed fairly quickly. Using pebble trays can help increase the humidity around your plants (this is always a good idea, especially in winter). These trays will prove to be a valuable addition to your houseplant collection. Here's why it's a good idea to use a pebble tray.

• A pebble tray allows the moisture in the tray to rise up around plants to create the humid conditions they need.
• The pebbles themselves keep the plants out of any water that collects in the bottom of the tray.
• The pebbles look good as a setting for your plants and will show them off.
• Some pebbles (such as white stone chips) will reflect the light back under the leaves of the plant and further increase plant growth.

If you live in a large city, even with plenty of window space, you may not have the bright light needed for most plants. This is because clean windows aren't easy to come by in areas where industrial fumes and car exhaust layer window surfaces. If you can clean your own windows, do it. In fact, do it several times during the year. It doesn't take long before the grime and dirt obscure visibility altogether. Your plants will be the first ones to tell you about it.

Many of us like to summer our houseplants outdoors in protected areas, such as in pergolas or arbors, under trees, or on sheltered, well-lit patios. It's a relief to let nature water and sun our plants after having done it ourselves all winter. They always look healthier and more vigorous by the time fall comes. But when fall temperatures begin to drop at night, start preparing the windows where plants will be placed.

To use a pebble tray correctly, simply set it underneath the light and put your plants on top of the pebbles. Make sure, however, that you keep the plants up on the pebbles—above the water—to prevent root rot. I like this idea because it makes for easy watering and no mess: The water simply drains out the drainage hole of each pot and flows into the pan of pebbles, creating humidity in the immediate area. Your plants will love this extra humidity and will return the favor by growing larger and more robust.

Here's a list of some good plants for artificial light gardening:
• Begonias
• Bromeliads
• Cinerarias
• *Cissus*, such as kangaroo vine (*C. antarctica*)
• Cyclamen
• *Episcia*, such as flame violet (*E. cupreata*)
• *Fittonia*, such as nerve plant (*F. verschaffeltii* var. *argyroneura*) and mosaic plant (*F. verschaffeltii*)
• Freckle-face or polka-dot plant (*Hypoestes phyllostachya*)
• Gesneriads, such as gloxinias, African violets, *Hypocyrta*, *Aeschynanthus*, and *Streptocarpus*
• Impatiens, such as *Impatiens wallerana*
• Moses-in-the-cradle (*Rhoeo spathacea*)
• Orchids
• Pellionia
• Peperomias
• Piggyback plant (*Tolmiea menziesii*)
• *Pilea*, such as friendship plant (*P. involucrata*) and aluminum plant (*P. cadierei*)
• Purple passion vine or velvet plant (*Gynura aurantiaca* 'Sarmentosa' or *G. aurantiaca*)
• *Rhoicissus*, such as grape ivy (*R. rhomboidea*)

African violets are excellent plants to grow under artificial lights.

• Saxifrages, such as strawberry geranium (*Saxifraga stolonifera*)
• Swedish Ivy (*Plectranthus australis*)
• Tradescantias

I'd like to share with you the story of how I came to appreciate the value of artificial lights. In the 1960s, when I first began my houseplant hobby, new and exciting plants came my way almost weekly. I often visited five or six plant stores (some of them small family businesses) in order to explore the variety of plants in my area. I also had an ulterior motive for choosing family-owned stores: Those people knew more about houseplants and their care than anyone at the chain stores or garden centers (today, the same is often true), and they didn't mind talking to you about plants. You could pick up pointers—little tricks that you wouldn't find in books.

One small shop I went back to on a regular basis was owned by a tiny white-haired woman who had to have been in her seventies. Her face was deeply lined

What kinds of pebbles should I use in my pebble trays?

Whatever you like. Here are some suggestions:
• Pea gravel
• Aquarium gravel
• Perlite
• White stone chips
• White quartz chips (These won't let fungi spores grow as easily as the other pebbles will.)

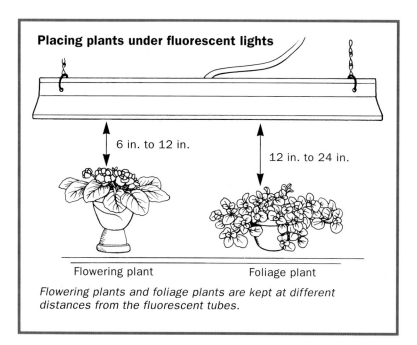

Placing plants under fluorescent lights

6 in. to 12 in.

12 in. to 24 in.

Flowering plant   Foliage plant

Flowering plants and foliage plants are kept at different distances from the fluorescent tubes.

Can I use regular incandescent bulbs to grow my plants instead of fluorescent tubes?

I wouldn't. The bulbs burn too hot for plants and can burn their leaves. I've seen leaves cooked after having sat for a few hours under incandescent bulbs. These bulbs are also too costly to burn for the number of hours required. They're just inefficient.

with age, but the minute she began talking about her plants, the years fell away as she grew animated with youthful enthusiasm. Her plants were always grown on benches—benches, benches everywhere; they filled the small shop entirely. Artificial light fixtures lined the growing spaces, giving a purple glow to the luxuriant foliage nestled in clay pots, which were lined up like sentries on damp sand.

On my first visit, I closely examined her plants, astounded at the leaf sizes, vibrant colors, vigorous growing habits, and overall sizes. She explained that the artificial light she used contained the colors of the light spectrum that plants need most for their peak development. I selected a rooted cutting, about 8 in. long, of a purple passion vine (*Gynura aurantiaca* 'Sarmentosa'). Removing it from its little pot, I saw the thick, white,

sturdy roots of a plant in vigorous growth—the thing was absolutely wallowing in good health.

I left the shop with the trunk of my car loaded, convinced that artificial light was good for plants.

I recommend artificial lighting for anyone in a small condo or apartment—not everyone is fortunate to have a balcony facing in the right direction. You can keep African violets in bloom most of the year by using lights. If you like fresh herbs for cooking during the winter, turn one of your kitchen cabinets into a growing area. And why stop there? You can turn any part of the house into an artificial-light growing area. In European countries, where space is often limited, indoor artificial-light gardening has been a popular hobby for decades.

Buying Fluorescent Tubes

Okay, let's say you'd like to try it. What do you look for in the stores? Fluorescent tubes; they come in all sizes. You may even see tubes made especially for growing plants—they produce the spectrum of light needed for excellent growth. These specialty tubes will cost more, but most growers will agree that the nonspecialty ones are just as good, and last longer.

You'll need a combination of cool-white and warm-white fluorescent tubes. Use two, four, six, or even eight, depending on what you're trying to do. They should be 40 watts each. Indoor gardening clubs used to recommend a 50/50 combination (cool white to warm white) for the best results, and I believe they still do. Now, remember that it's the intensity of the light that's important when growing houseplants indoors. This means that you need several tubes to bring flowering plants into bloom. Fewertubes are needed for foliage plants, for which intensity is not that important.

Don't worry if you don't have the money to shell out for the specialty fluorescent tubes. Many professional growers don't use anything but the cool-white/warm-white combination, and they're still producing an excellent product. Their plants must be good enough for the public, or they'd be out of business. So, expensive specialty tubes aren't really needed. Does that mean that garden writers don't endorse them? No. There are certainly some writers who not only endorse these bulbs but also use them. But my experience has been that you can get the same results without spending lots of money.

Setting Up the System

Once you get everything hooked up, you're ready to set your plants under the lights. Set flowering plants 6 in. to 12 in. away from the tubes and set foliage plants 12 in. to 24 in. away. You may have to tweak the system until you get the light distance set the way your plants prefer it, but they can be placed as close as 6 in. from the light without burning (we're talking about fluorescent lights here). The general rule is the closer the light source, the better the growth. You certainly can grow luxuriant plants with two tubes, but more would be better.

You'll need to leave the lights turned on ten to twelve hours a day. This means that you'll have to water and feed more often, because your plants will be exposed to light for longer periods of time and they'll be growing faster than if you used natural light. They'll be hungrier and thirstier than your plants that are clustered around a picture window. This is because plants under tubes transpire (lose water through their leaves) more often, and that water has to be replaced. They'll also be undergoing more cell growth at a faster pace, and this process will require more food.

You'll find that some plants grow better under lights than others. If there is a houseplant club in your area, you may benefit from attending a few meetings. Some members in the group will certainly be growing plants under lights, and can give you some ideas. These knowledgeable people know all the latest on growing plants this way, and you may find yourself a member before long. Often, club members are invited to one another's homes to view their collections. This has its advantages, as you can see the plants and the growing conditions firsthand. In addition, club members stay in touch with one another and pass around all the latest information on various indoor-gardening subjects. They even may ask lecturers to speak to them about indoor growing under lights.

If there isn't a club, start one with a few interested artificial-light gardeners. There are also plenty of home-project books on the market that'll instruct you on tube installation and provide you with plans for a build-it-yourself cabinet or bench. Just look around, and you can find everything you need without going to too much trouble.

These plants are excellent candidates for a north window or a spot in your house with little light (from back to front): snake plant (*Sansevieria trifasciata*), pothos (*Epipremnum aureum*), Chinese evergreen (*Aglaonema modestum*), and bird's-nest fern (*Asplenium nidus*).

Plants for a north-facing window

If you have a north-facing window, you can grow a lot more plants than you think. Try any of these plants in shade and semishade exposures:

- Bird's-nest fern (*Asplenium nidus*)
- Cast-iron plant (*Aspidistra elatior* 'Variegata')
- Castor-oil plant (*Ricinus communis*)
- Chinese evergreen (*Aglaonema modestum*)
- Cordylines (*Agavaceae* family)
- Ferns
- Fittonias
- Goosefoot plant, arrowhead vine, or nephthytis (*Syngonium podophyllum*)
- Peace lily (*Spathiphyllum*); the small varieties will fit on a windowsill, the large Mauna Loa is floor-sized.
- Philodendron; there are several species in this genus
- Piggyback plant (*Tolmiea menziesii*)
- Prayer plant (*Maranta leuconeura kerchoviana*)
- Snake plant (*Sansevieria trifasciata*)

Changing fluorescent tubes

Unfortunately, your tubes won't last forever. They begin to burn out slowly from their ends after about one year of use. Yes, you can burn them longer, but the light won't be as intense. The light will be strongest toward the center of the tube, so you'll come out better if you use long tubes; but you may not be able to house such a setup. Just to give you a reference point here, commercial growers use 48-in. tubes.

Don't wait until your tubes burn out to change them. You should put in new ones every year. Some gardeners change them every 18 months, but they notice that plant growth is not as good. Here's a tip that'll save you money: Change the tubes in staggered succession, not all at the same time. Here's why: You'll run into some expense if you change all of them at the same time (save your money for plants). And you may burn your plants if you put in all new tubes at the same time, because the plants have been used to the diminishing light over the year. Putting them under a new set of tubes is equivalent to setting them in direct sunlight.

Without water, plants die—they're composed mostly of water. Water helps to transport much-needed sugars and other materials throughout the plant's structure. And it's in a constant state of flux; that is, water levels are always changing, going up or down, as the plant's needs change (based on the environment: soil, wind, sun, season, etc.).

A good example of this takes place on a hot day. The sun causes moisture needs within the plant to increase, and some of the water escapes through the leaves. This means that more water must be drawn out of the soil by the plant's roots and transported to the parts of the plant needing it most.

How Plants Die from Underwatering

If the soil is dry, the plant will begin to use its own water. This means that water is removed from the plant's own cells and placed at its disposal. If water is still not forthcoming, cellular collapse takes place. In other words, the plant wilts.

At this point, if water is still not available, the plant's resources are spent, cellular collapse is complete, and the plant dies.

Most plants will recover if they're caught in time and given the water they need. When this happens, water is replaced first in the plant cells and then in other areas. Then, within a few hours, the plant revives. But there are some plants that will not rejuvenate after cellular collapse. The herb rosemary is one. If it's ever allowed to go dry, it *never* regains cellular resilience in some of its parts. Some branches will become dry and soon die.

This presents a problem, especially if your rosemary plant has been shaped into a "tree." Rosemary is a good subject for training and clipping into a little tree form—the process is called "topiary." But if some of the branches of the tree die due to bone-dry soil, the shape of the topiary is destroyed; and the plant must be shaped all over again—a process that could take a few years.

How Plants Die from Overwatering

When a plant is overwatered, its roots die because of root rot. Plant roots need oxygen just as we do. They get oxygen

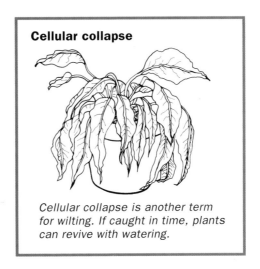

Cellular collapse

Cellular collapse is another term for wilting. If caught in time, plants can revive with watering.

The best test for your plant's watering needs isn't a complicated machine—it's your own finger. Insert it into the soil up to the first knuckle to test for soil moisture.

when the plant has had its water and begins to dry out. As the root ball dries out, it takes on oxygen and prepares for the next watering. In most instances, it's better to leave a plant a little dry than to leave it wet all the time. Wet all the time means the roots don't get air, and root rot begins.

The excess water you pour into the pot when watering should drain out within a matter of minutes. If it doesn't, you've got trouble. Your soil is too heavy, and the best thing you can do for your plant is to repot it using a much better, lighter, and more porous potting soil, which will allow the water to moisten the root ball while letting the excess water drain out.

But not all potting soils are created equal; so look closely at what you're buying. I used potting soil that was too heavy in my beginner days as a houseplant gardener. At that time, there weren't many books to advise me. What

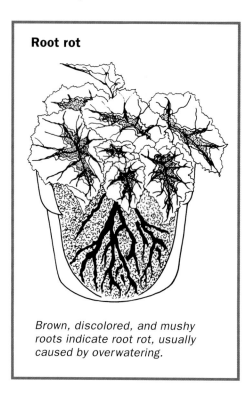

Root rot

Brown, discolored, and mushy roots indicate root rot, usually caused by overwatering.

you want is a soil with perlite, peat moss, and other good things added to make it more porous. Heavy soil won't let water drain out of the pot—it stays in and around the root ball, preventing air from getting to plant roots.

If you don't know which soil is best for your kind of plant, consult the salespeople at a family-owned garden store. They'll take the time to explain things to you. And they know what they're doing—they use the good stuff to pot their own plants, which they sell to the public. They usually keep what they use on hand all the time. Take a look at it to see what good potting soil should look like. These stores always have the better commercial potting soil for sale in plastic bags as well. It is usually sold in 20- and 40-pound bags.

How to Tell if a Plant Needs Watering

Now, about that brown thumb of yours. Did you know that improper watering kills more houseplants than anything else? You don't need expensive meters to measure moisture in the soil, and you don't need to guess at your plant's water needs. Put your finger in the soil—it's the only surefire way to determine if you should water. Here's how:
• Stick your finger into the soil a little beyond the first knuckle.
• If the soil feels damp, don't water.
• If the soil feels dry, water.

Experienced houseplant gardeners use another method to gauge dry soil, and it works especially well for plants in clay pots: They pick up the pot. If the pot is heavy, they know they shouldn't water. If the pot is light, they water. But the best course of action for beginners is the old finger-in-the-soil method until they get the feel of detecting the water needs of their plants.

This watering method ensures that plants don't receive too much water and stay wet all the time. Remember, over-watering is the number one reason most houseplants die.

The Correct Way to Water

There are two ways you can water: from the top and from the bottom. Whichever way you water, make sure that the plant is thoroughly watered and then allowed to dry out a bit before it's watered again. Water well, but not often. This is the trick to good watering practices. When you think it's time to water again, make sure you're correct in your hunch by sticking your finger down into the soil.

Watering from the top

Here's the way to water your plants from the top:

1. Check the soil of each plant to see if it needs watering. Your finger should scratch into the soil up to the first knuckle. If the pot is large, bury your finger deeper into the soil.

2. Add water if the soil is dry. Pour the water gently, in an even stream. Don't hesitate to flood the pot.

3. Look for water draining out the bottom. Keep watering until you see water flowing from the hole in the bottom of the pot. Then go on to the next pot.

4. If you have saucers under your pots, empty them. Empty them again if they still contain water after a half-hour.

There are three methods of watering from the top: taking plants to the sink, leaving them where they are, and taking them to the bathtub.

Taking the plants to the sink always worked for me when I lived in an apartment. It's just the thing for small plants. The kitchen floor was linoleum and didn't mind being splashed. While at the sink, it's imperative to check each plant all over for any insect or disease problems that may be developing.

If your plants are too big to move, water them where they are. Water them on the floor or table where they sit, allowing the water to seep slowly into the saucer under each plant.

Taking your plants to the bathtub is really helpful for plants too big for the sink. If they're in plastic containers and in a soilless mix, they may be light enough for you to tote. The bathroom offers three advantages over the other suggested methods:

• You have room to move about and inspect plants for insects.

I've heard that I should never water with cold water. Is this true?

Yes. Have you ever plunged into the cold water of a swimming pool? Quite a shock, isn't it? Well, it's the same for plants. They hate cold water. Roots could be damaged, and water spots are sometimes left on the leaves once they dry—and the spots don't come off.

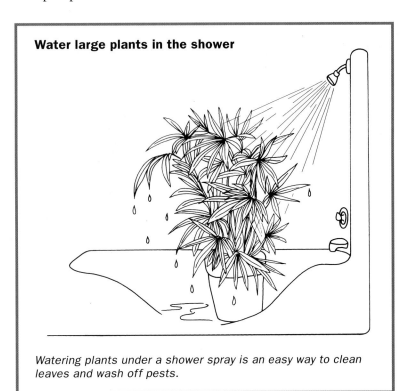

Water large plants in the shower

Watering plants under a shower spray is an easy way to clean leaves and wash off pests.

- You can clean leaves or wash off any insect pests under a torrent of water by using the tap, a shower spray, or a hand-held sprayer.
- You can effortlessly water any large plants at the same time you are inspecting them.

Regardless of the watering method you choose, while you're near the plant,

Watering by immersion

Watering by immersion ensures that soil gets a thorough soaking.

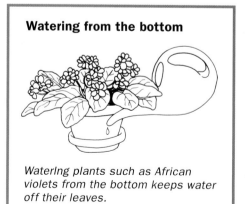

Watering from the bottom

Watering plants such as African violets from the bottom keeps water off their leaves.

inspect it for insect or rot problems. You can't do this properly without putting your hands on the plant.
- Part the leaves and look at stems.
- Look under the leaves for signs of webbing or discoloration.
- Look into the crown of the plant (down into the center) for die-back or misshapen new growth.
- Take any plant you are concerned about out of its pot and look at the roots. They should be thick, plump, resilient, and (usually) white.

It's imperative that you come in contact with your plants in order to find out what's going on with them.

Watering from the bottom
Watering from the bottom is used for African violets, gloxinias, cyclamens, and any plant that doesn't want its foliage wet. Since these plants don't like their leaves or crowns damp, bottom watering suits them well. You also can use this method for plants that you've allowed to get too dry. Here's how:

1. Fill a bucket with warm water and immerse the pot to just below the pot rim.

2. Allow the pot to sit in the water until the soil surface looks wet. Overly dry plants should soak in warm water until the surface is wet—this may take a while, perhaps 15 minutes.

3. Remove the pot from the water, and allow it to drain.

Rather than using this immersion technique, some houseplant gardeners simply put water in the saucer and let the plant wick it up into the pot from below. Pour out any water left in the plant's saucer after 15 minutes.

Judging How Often to Water

Generally, the larger the leaf surface and the more rapid the rate of growth, the more water the plant needs. But now you know that there's only one surefire way to tell if a plant needs water—stick your finger down into the soil and see if it's dry. Here are a few other things to keep in mind to determine how often to water a plant.

- **The size of the plant.** If the plant is large, you'll be watering a lot. It'll have a large root ball, which will demand more water, more often. But if the plant is small, it won't need to be watered often because it'll have a smaller root ball.
- **The size of the pot.** A large plant in a small pot needs more water than a smaller plant in the same size pot. This is because there isn't enough soil in the pot to hold excess water and keep the roots evenly moist—most of the pot is filled with roots. You'll find yourself watering this fellow often, and you may even want to transfer the plant into a larger pot (only 1 in. larger) to relieve you from having to make the necessary trips to the sink. Does the plant need repotting? A plant that hasn't been repotted in a few years and which has outgrown its quarters needs more water.
- **The plant's growth.** Any plant in active growth will need more water. Active growth means new roots are being made, and new top growth is being added. All of this activity requires more water because the transpiration rate is also being stepped up. Growing things get thirsty (they also get hungry, as you'll see in Chapter 6).
- **The type of pot.** *Clay pots* absorb water—this is because clay is porous. Both air and water pass through the sides of a clay pot continually. This

means that the plant will dry out faster and that you'll be watering more often. *Plastic pots* are not porous, and the soil around the roots of your plant will stay moist longer. Because of this, it's easy to overwater your plant if it's in a plastic pot. (More about pots in Chapter 7.)
- **The type of potting soil.** If you're growing cacti and your potting soil is mostly sand, you will have to water more often—sand is porous and doesn't hold water. But if the soil is the usual good houseplant potting soil (there *is* some bad potting soil out there), it will hold water longer, which means that you won't have to water so often. (See Chapter 4 for more on soil.)
- **The time of year.** Plants need more water in the summer for two reasons: They're actively growing, and the air is warmer (they transpire more). Plants need less water in the winter for two

Clay pots come in a variety of shapes and sizes. They are favored by many for their classic appearance, but because they're porous, you'll find yourself watering more often.

Plastic pots are colorful and keep water from evaporating, which means less-frequent watering. The pot in the center is a self-watering pot.

reasons: They're usually in their rest cycle (they're dormant), and winter days aren't that sunny.

- **The type of plant.** Some plants want to stand in water because that's how they grow in their native environment. Others prefer to be bone dry, like cacti. Still others, such as the tropicals (monsteras, palms, philodendrons, scheffleras, dieffenbachias, chlorophytums, and begonias, for example), like to go through a moist/dry period. They want their roots moist and don't want any more water until the soil dries out a bit.
- **The plant's stems and leaves.** Does the plant have thick, fleshy stems or leaves? If so, they will hold water longer, which means you'll water *less* often. Does your plant have thin stems and small or thin leaves? If so, it will need watering *more* often because the leaves and stems won't hold excess water for use during dry periods.

- **The site of the plant.** If the plant is in a south- or west-facing window where it receives sun for several hours, it'll dry out relatively fast, even during the winter months. The same plant set farther away from the window at the same time of the year will not dry out as fast. This is because the farther away from the window you go, the less light there is for plant growth or sun-dried soil.
- **The temperature in your home.** If you keep your home well heated in winter (say about 76°F or higher), plants will dry out quickly. But if the temperature is lower (65°F, for example), plants will remain moister longer.
- **The state of bloom.** If your plant is about to come into flower or if it's already flowering, it will use much more water than it did when it was producing only leaves.

Double-Potting

Double-potting allows you to cover a plain pot by slipping it into a more decorative pot. But gardeners don't do this only for ornamental reasons. Double-potting adds humidity to a plant's environment because moisture from the sphagnum moss packed between the two pots is absorbed by the plant. Thus, double-potting allows a plant to go longer without being watered.

Here's how to double-pot:

1. Select a pot larger than the one your plant is currently in. The large pot does not need a drainage hole.

Double-potting

1. Place the potted plant in a larger pot.

2. Soak sphagnum moss in warm water, and squeeze most of the water out.

3. Pack moss between the pots.

4. Keep the moss moist.

2. Set your potted plant in the center of the large pot.

3. Soak long-fiber sphagnum moss in warm water for 15 minutes. Use a little moss at a time, since it swells as it absorbs water.

4. Wring most of the water out of the moss.

5. Pack the moist sphagnum in the space between the two pots.

6. Keep this packing moist, but not wet, at all times.

Some people use peat moss for double-potting because it holds more moisture longer. But if peat ever gets dry, you'll have to scrape it out and then water it down to remoisten it. Sphagnum moss is better for this job.

Splashes of cold water caused the discoloration on these leaves.

Watering Don'ts

Now, let's gather all of the things we've learned so far about how not to water, and make a list. Become acquainted with this list over time, and the number one killer of houseplants—overwatering— will not be one of your worries.

• **Don't water plants on a schedule.** Don't get into the habit of watering just because it's Saturday morning. *There should always be a reason to water.* Water after sticking a finger down into the soil to see if it's dry. If the soil isn't dry, don't water.

• **Never just sprinkle the soil with a little water.** This does no good at all. Plants need *deep* watering. Then they must be allowed to go a little dry before their next watering so that air can get to the roots.

• **When a plant looks sick, don't water it (and don't feed it, either).** It has enough to worry about without having to digest food and deal with wet soil. A hot meal and warm drinks may help *you* when you're sick, but watering and feeding won't help sick plants. They add to their stress.

• **Don't water African violets (or any fuzzy-leaf plant), cyclamens, or begonias from above.** These plants don't like water on their leaves or in their crowns (the center of the plant where the leaves come out). They'll rot if water stands in these areas.

• **Don't let plants constantly sit in water unless they do it in their native environment.** Most plants don't want wet feet at all. Always remember to empty their saucers 15 to 30 minutes after you've watered them. If the plants sit in water for long enough, they'll get root rot.

• **Don't water your plants only from the bottom.** Except for the plants mentioned previously (African violets,

Watering danger signals at a glance

The wilted and brown foliage of this plant are signs of underwatering.

Signs of overwatering

- *The leaves are limp and soft; there may be rotten areas and poor growth.*
- *Flowers are moldy.*
- *New and old leaves fall off the plant.*
- *Leaves have brown tips on the ends; and they curl, yellow, and wilt.*

Signs of underwatering

- *The leaves are limp and wilted; there is little or no new leaf growth.*
- *Flowers fall off or the color fades quickly.*
- *The oldest leaves fall off first, then the others.*
- *The lower leaves have brown, dry edges; they curl, yellow, and wilt.*

cyclamens, and begonias), water from the top every now and then to flush the salts and fertilizers from the pot. Bottom watering causes salts to form on the soil's surface and sit there; and some of these salts can damage plants if they accumulate around the rim of the pot, where the plants' leaves may rest.

- **Don't water plants with cold water.** Use only warm water. If cold water sits on leaves, it usually spots them. These unsightly spots appropriately are called "water spots," and they won't wash off.
- **Don't water your plants at night— especially in the winter.** Water them in the morning. This way, the soil won't be wet at nighttime. Many problems beset plants when they're kept wet at night, and fungus is one of them.
- **Don't buy an expensive soil moisture meter.** The best detector of soil moisture is your own finger. Save your money to buy plants.

TIPS

Using rainwater

Ages ago (when I lived in an apartment), I can remember standing out in a storm, with my umbrella and a pitcher, catching rainwater as it rushed through the downspout. I was growing bromeliads at the time and used rainwater because I had better luck with it than with tap water. You can collect tons of rainwater in no time this way and store it in huge barrels (mosquito-proof it by putting a lid on top). Some catalog companies sell a large plastic barrel especially designed for this purpose.

Rainwater fertilizes plants because it contains some nitrogen if it's used soon after it's been collected. But rainwater isn't what it used to be for some people.

If you live in a heavily industrialized area, you may want to stick with tap water—it's probably more pure than your rainwater. I live in the country, which means that the air is fresh, clean, and clear all the time. The rainwater probably is, too. I've never noticed any ill effects from using it on my plants.

Shower your plants

Showering your plants is done for health reasons, but it's also done to raise the humidity around the plants for a brief period. Insects are just as plentiful indoors as they are outdoors, and a good lathering in the shower kills them. There really is nothing better at killing insects than soap and water.

Try this remedy:

1. Mix 1 teaspoon of mild liquid dish-washing soap in 1 gallon of warm water.

2. Pour some of the liquid into a mister bottle.

3. Spray the leaves of your plants—over and under.

4. Gently rub the mixture on the leaves.

5. Let the plants sit for about 15 minutes.

6. Rinse the plants.

After the soapy water is sprayed on, I gently work the soap around (being careful because some leaves tear easily) to catch insects and clean leaves of dust and grease. If your plant room is near a kitchen, you won't believe the grease that gets on plant leaves just from everyday cooking!

When the plant is soaped well, I let the mixture sit on the leaves for 15 minutes. Then I rinse off the soap with warm water from the overhead shower spray. I set the plant on some old towels to drain briefly before returning it to its place in the plant room. I don't bother drying the leaves, because this moisture will increase the humidity for any plants in the immediate area.

Not all plants will allow you to handle them this way. You can't shower cacti or some succulents, for example. Your experience will tell you which plants are too fragile for this kind of treatment.

You may not have realized it, but plants are just as sensitive to temperature as humans are. Remember how you feel when the temperature soars during a summer heat wave? Your body slows down, the air feels oppressive, and you don't want to do much of anything. The same is true of plants. Many outdoor plants simply shut down when the temp gets too high. Some vegetables won't even set bud when the temperature is in the 90s. They either remain in a holding pattern for a while or just give up and fall to the ground.

And what about winter? If you have pots lined up along the windowsill to catch the winter light, you may be contributing to their death. In cold weather, the temperature close to the glass of a single-paned window will drop 10°F or more below room temperature. The rest of the room temperature will be higher, of course. But plants left to press against the glass on a cold night may be frostbitten by morning. (If you are lucky enough to have double-paned glass, you won't have to worry.)

Consider this for a minute: Most houseplants are tropicals, and they grow best within a temperature range of 75°F during the daytime to 60°F at night. Some prefer a greater nightly dip in temperature to 55° to 50°F. There are growers who feel that even 75°F is too high for a daytime temp—they prefer 68°F. Whatever the case, houseplants are resilient to some extent and can endure temperatures slightly above or below the preferred range for short periods.

Whatever the argument, houseplants *do* seem to like the 10° to 15°F drop in temperature at night, and some of them won't bloom unless they get it.

Here are three (out of many) good examples of what I mean. First, several years ago I lived in Mississippi, a place noted for its heavenly perfumed gardenias. Huge shrubs were everywhere on

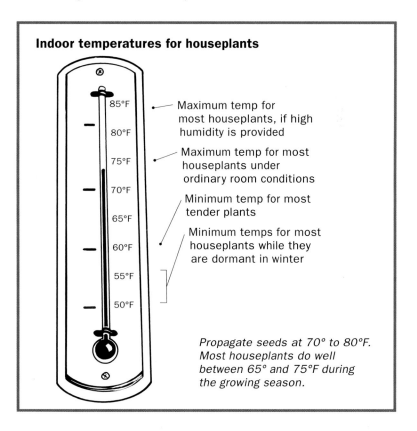

Indoor temperatures for houseplants

85°F
80°F — Maximum temp for most houseplants, if high humidity is provided
75°F — Maximum temp for most houseplants under ordinary room conditions
70°F
65°F — Minimum temp for most tender plants
60°F — Minimum temps for most houseplants while they are dormant in winter
55°F
50°F

Propagate seeds at 70° to 80°F. Most houseplants do well between 65° and 75°F during the growing season.

Christmas cactus puts on a beautiful display of color after it has experienced cool night temperatures. (Photo by Derek Fell.)

the plant's pollinators), as well as the size of the huge bloom (a moth or a bat can't miss it). The plant must act fast if it's to ensure its survival, because in a few short hours, the bloom will be dead.

The third example of how temperature affects a plant's bloom cycle is the Christmas cactus (*Epiphyllum* hybrids or *Schlumbergera bridgesii*— take your pick). It needs a few weeks of cool temps in the fall to trigger bud set. And then when it does set bud, you have to be careful moving it around the house when you bring it in. Sometimes it drops all of its swollen buds if moved from room to room too often.

It's a real heartbreaker to see this. The buds become soft, and when you touch them, they fall. This is because each room has its own temperature, and each part of a room has its own temperature. Microclimates are all over your house, and the plant simply can't dance to such rapid changes.

So, as you see, temperature is more crucial to some plants than to others. Even in the house, 85°F is usually the maximum temperature for most houseplants. They won't thrive indoors in temps above 85°F unless humidity is provided. A plunge in temperature also should be avoided—it can be fatal. The exceptions here, of course, are cacti and succulents.

Cacti (and, to some extent, succulents) are used to hot days and cold nights in their desert environments; these variations are mere child's play to them. But look at how they've evolved to handle the great discrepancy in temp. Instead of leaves, they have needles. Instead of transpiring their moisture each hour as most plants do, they've developed an ingenious system of water

What are some of the danger signals that tell me I'm growing my plants at the wrong temperature?

- If the temp is too cold, the leaves will curl; then they'll turn brown and fall off.

- If the temp is too hot, the lower leaves will wilt and their edges will turn brown; the bottom leaves will fall off. Flowers will live for only a short time. You'll get spindly growth in the winter and summer if the temperature is too high. This will result even if you have good light.

- If there is a sudden temperature change, the leaves will fall off after quickly turning yellow.

the property, and I used to look forward to when the night temperature would drop to 60°F, because I knew the buds would begin to set, and fragrant gardenias would soon fill the house with their spicy perfume.

Those of you who have a night-blooming cereus (either *Epiphyllum oxypetalum* or *Hylocereus undatus*) know what I'm about to use for the second example. The buds of this plant swell to a certain point but then remain in a holding pattern until the night temp drops to 50° to 60°F. If the cool nights don't come within a few weeks, the buds shrivel and die. But if the temperature does drop, the buds begin to develop their long stems and finally burst into the most exquisite flowers imaginable.

Temperature is critical for this plant (and for the houseplant gardener), because it blooms *only* at night and *only* for a few hours. In its native environment, during this brief period, the bloom must attract night-flying moths or bats so that the plant can be pollinated. That's where the potent fragrance comes in (it's meant to travel a good distance to lure conservation: They store it because rainfall is scarce. It's amazing how living things will adapt in order to survive.

Tricks for Managing Temperature

By this time, you've realized that most houseplants grow better within a narrow range of temperatures. And, if you think about it, humans prefer the same temperature range: 55° to 75°F is agreeable to most people. But people can shed or don clothing to adjust to even greater extremes in temperature. Plants can do this to some extent to deal with extreme heat. Here's how it works.

Plants depend on moisture rising through their roots and into the leaves in order to cool down (similar to the way we perspire to cool our bodies). In very high temperatures of 90° to 100°F over a long period, plants will shut down completely and begin conserving moisture by dropping their leaves. I've seen trees do this during summers when the temperature stays in the 90s and 100s for weeks on end and no rain falls. Because the leaves require water and the tree isn't getting any, it simply drops all of its leaves to conserve what water it has—that's survival. Once the rains return, a new set of leaves is grown to continue normal photosynthesis. During severe drought, I've seen trees acquire two or three sets of new leaves in one season. Ingenious.

High temperature

Indoors The real problem in keeping houseplants in a room with a high temperature is that the humidity falls (more about humidity in Chapter 5). If you can raise the humidity *as the temp rises,* everything will be fine. But you won't be. Talk about a sticky jungle atmosphere! This is what's done at botanical gardens for the tropical plants. The greenhouse temp soars; but the

humidity is also increased, so the plants don't mind it so much. Steamy is okay for them. But try working in an atmosphere like this or even walking through it slowly while looking at the plants. Before long, you can't wait to get outdoors!

What tricks can you use to deal with a plant's natural response to high temperature?

- **Use pebble trays.** This is a practical way for you and your plants to remain comfortable in the heat. Pebble trays increase the humidity around the plant's immediate area from the bottom. Plants are placed on their saucers and both are set into shallow waterproof trays (2 in. to 3 in. tall) that have been filled to 1 in. with pebbles. Water is added to the pebbles (and not allowed to dry out). Plants must *never* be in touch with the water. Keep them above it. Placing the pots on saucers

In a greenhouse's closed environment, consistent temperature and humidity can be maintained.

African violets should always be watered from the bottom, and a pebble tray can be used to increase humidity. (Photo by Derek Fell.)

Group plants to raise humidity

Plants grouped together maintain a more consistent temperature because they share each other's humidity.

ensures that the plants' roots won't grow down into the pebbles. As the temp in the room rises, the water in the tray warms and humidity around the plants rises, keeping *them* cool— and *you* dry.

- **Group plants with similar humidity needs.** Plants transpire—lose water— through the pores in their leaves. Have you ever seen drops of water on the tips of some plants? Transpiration has taken place. If you group together plants with similar humidity needs, the transpiration and the moist soil in each pot will raise the humidity in the immediate area.

Make sure, however, that you don't include cacti with your grouping. They aren't used to humidity. Tropical plants (and most houseplants are tropicals) like 50 to 70 percent humidity. Desert plants are used to a humidity of only 10 to 30 percent. You don't want them rotting. In fact, why don't you grow your cacti and succulents off by themselves? Botanical gardens do this to keep both tropical and desert plants happy.

A word of caution: Plants that are packed too tightly together share more than humidity. They can share fungi and insect pests (more about this in Chapter 8). Make sure air can circulate in between foliage and pots.

- **Double-pot.** Double-potting involves setting the potted plant into a larger waterproof container or pot and filling in the space between the two pots with damp sphagnum long-fiber moss (see Chapter 2 for details). This moss packing is kept moist and helps raise the humidity around the plant. It also keeps plant roots cool. I use this method with only a few of my plants, since it's expensive to buy so many different pots.

• **Mist.** This old standby also is used to raise the humidity in the immediate area around the plant. Mister bottles are easy to find, cost a few dollars, fit into the curve of the hand, and are easy to use at a moment's notice. Misting involves covering the entire plant in a thin veil of mist. Doing this a few times each day adds the humidity you need for several hours.

A word of caution: If you mist, do it in the morning and afternoon hours. Misting in the evening only sets the plant up for fungus and rot problems. I don't like misting. The carpet and everything around the plant (walls, furniture, magazines) stay too moist to suit me. You'll have to be your own judge here.

Outdoors Protecting plants that summer outdoors is easy. Here are a few ways to protect them from high temperatures:

• **Hose 'em down.** If you summer your plants outdoors, this method will be convenient. Naturally, plants should be placed out of direct sunlight and in a fairly bright, sheltered area, but that doesn't mean they won't get hot. Spraying them off lightly (all over) with a hose is an excellent, trouble-free way to drop the temp around your plants. In a sheltered area, the humidity will hang around for quite a while, and the plants will love it.

A word of caution: Don't turn the hose on full force. There are so many neat gadgets out now that diffuse the water so that the full force of its rushing through the hose is broken. You want a drenching mist here, not a drenching torrent. There's a difference.

• **Puddle the patio.** You also can do this in conjunction with hosing your plants to make sure that the humidity stays around for most of the day. I use this method all summer, because our summer temp stays in the 90s and many times it's in the 100s. In the morning during the hot months of July, August, September, and part of October (I live in the South), I spray off the foliage and then make puddles of water around the pots. During the day, I may refresh the puddles if it hasn't rained.

But, once again, a word of caution: Don't wet the foliage at night. You're asking for fungus and rot problems if you do.

Low temperature

When your furnace kicks in for the winter, the humidity plummets drastically, and you have a new set of problems. How can you remain comfortably warm while keeping dormant plants at the lower temperature they like? How can you also keep the humidity up during this resting cycle?

Don't worry, it's not difficult. Here are some suggestions:

• Use your pebble trays
• Double-pot
• Mist
• Use an electric humidifier

Use the type of humidifier that you may already be using in your child's sickroom. It sends clouds of warm steam into the air around your plants without wetting their leaves. And this is certainly an advantage, because you don't want plant foliage staying wet for long during the winter. See Chapter 5 for more benefits of this handy appliance.

I've heard that you shouldn't set plants in front of an air-conditioner. Is this true?

Yes. Aside from the temperature's being much cooler than the plant is used to in its native environment, it also causes transpiration at a faster rate. Any wind blowing over leaves causes an increase in the plant's demand for water.

Heat from Radiators

If you have radiator heat in the winter, you can set up an attractive display of plants. Radiators are handy because they're usually just below or even with a window—where light is always accessible to plants.

Here's a setup you will want to try above your radiator:

- Use metal brackets wide enough to hold a thick wooden shelf and set them firmly into the wall up about 6 in. from the top of the radiator. You don't want the shelf to come in contact with the radiator itself.

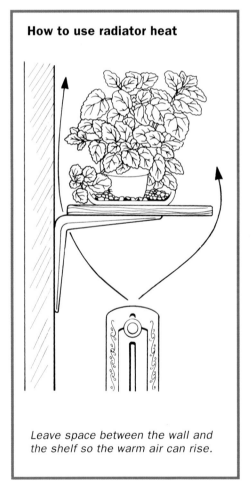

How to use radiator heat

Leave space between the wall and the shelf so the warm air can rise.

- Leave a space between the wall and the wood so that warm air can rise from the back behind the shelf.
- Allow the wooden shelf to overhang the front and back of the radiator by at least 6 in. This is to protect the plants from being cooked as the heat comes up and over the shelf edge.
- Prepare a pebble tray as discussed earlier. Set the pebble tray on the shelf and add your plants.

Plants love this bottom heat. You'll have excellent growing conditions, especially with the humidity from the pebble tray.

Heat from Windows

So far, we've been talking about heat from outdoors, indoors, furnaces, and radiators. But, we haven't said anything about the heat from a window.

Heat from a south-facing window can cook plants in the summer if they're close enough to the glass. This is because the light coming through is converted to heat. Remember those hot car seats in the summer? Play it safe by doing one of these:

- Place plants farther back from a south-facing window.
- Open the window to let in any available breezes.
- Place a fan in the area to cool it down.
- Hang a sheer curtain between the plant and the window.
- Hang a regular curtain in the same position, but close it during the hottest part of the day.
- Add humidity to ameliorate the heat.

These may seem like expensive ways to accommodate your plants, but remember that you have an investment to protect—especially if you own a lot of plants.

Other growers face the same problems. Think about greenhouse gardeners for a minute. People who own greenhouses have to make sure that they're vented in summer. Large commercial operations have a thermostated setup that kicks in, turning on a fan when the heat inside the greenhouse approaches a certain temperature—usually 75°F. In addition, the glass is usually painted over or shade cloth is applied during the hottest parts of the season so that the intense light doesn't burn tender foliage.

If you have your plants in a sunroom, you're probably getting bright light in high summer. Don't keep your plants right up against the glass. They can get foliage burns. Instead, think about installing pleated shades, which diffuse the light so that it's not so intense. The shades can be lowered during the day when the sun is most intense. This is the way I solved the light and heat problem in my sunroom. I stay a little cooler, too.

A Word about Hanging Plants

Do you have hanging plants in your home? You may not realize it, but the temperature is higher near the ceiling in summer and winter.

If you keep your home at 75°F in the winter, it's much warmer toward the ceiling than down where you're standing.

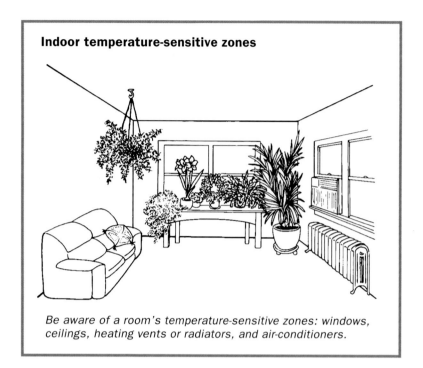

Indoor temperature-sensitive zones

Be aware of a room's temperature-sensitive zones: windows, ceilings, heating vents or radiators, and air-conditioners.

Is it any wonder that those ferns you've been hanging in the garden room for the winter soon get brown leaves, which end up falling off?

The remedy is simple: Increase the humidity for your hanging plants. Remember, humidity offsets high temperatures.

If you don't increase the humidity, you'll see brown leaf tips. Misting is fine, but you won't be able to supply enough moisture for a very long time. Use an electric humidifier; it will solve your problem.

Last summer, I left a plant in my car and went into a store to do some shopping. A few hours later I discovered the corpse—my plant was limp and never recovered. What happened?

Heat happened. The heat in a car in the middle of summer can reach 120°F or more. Plants are living things, and their "body" temperature is just like yours—it can take only so much heat.

Plants that hate the cold shoulder

There are some plants that just hate to get cold. They're called "cold-sensitive plants" for good reason: If the temp drops too low (below 50°F), they drop—dead. Give these tender plants warmer room conditions and don't put them into unheated rooms for the winter.

- African violets (*Saintpaulia ionantha*)
- Begonias (*Begonia* species)
- Bird-of-paradise (*Strelitzia reginae*)
- Bromeliads (*Bromelia* species)
- Calamondin (*Citrofortunella mitis*)
- Cape jasmine (*Gardenia jasminoides*)
- Cape primrose (*Streptocarpus* × *hybridus*)
- Chenille plant (*Acalypha hispida*)
- Cigar plant (*Cuphea ignea*)
- Clog plant (*Nematanthus glabra*)
- Crown-of-thorns (*Euphorbia milii* var. *splendens*)
- Egyptian star (*Pentas lanceolata*)
- Firecracker flower (*Crossandra infundibulicormis*)
- Flame-of-the-woods (*Ixora coccinea*)
- Flame violet (*Episcia cupreata*)
- Flamingo flower (*Anthurium scherzeranum*)
- Geraniums (*Pelargonium* species)
- Glory-bower or bleeding-heart vine (*Clerodendrum thomsoniae*)
- Goldfish plant (*Columnea* × *banksii* and *C. gloriosa*)
- Hibiscus (*Hibiscus rosa-sinensis*)
- Impatiens (*Impatiens* species and varieties)
- Jasmine (*Jasminum officinale*)
- Kalanchoe or flaming Katy (*Kalanchoe integra*)
- King's-crown (*Justicia carnea*)
- Lace-flower (*Episcia dianthiflora*)
- Lantana (*Lantana camara*)
- Lipstick plant (*Aeschynanthus pulcher*)
- Mandevilla (*Mandevilla sanderi*)
- Natal plum (*Carissa grandiflora*)
- Night jessamine (*Cestrum nocturnum*)
- Some orchids
- Peace lily (*Spathiphyllum*)
- Plumbago or cape leadwort (*Plumbago auriculata*)
- Polka-dot (*Hypoestes phyllostachya*)
- Yesterday-today-and-tomorrow (*Brunfelsia australia*)
- Zebra plant (*Aphelandra squarrosa* 'Brockfeld' and *A. squarrosa* 'Louisae')

Transporting plants in cold weather

Most houseplants (which are tropicals) are sensitive to cold. We buy poinsettias in winter (these are tropicals) for the Christmas season, carry them around outside in freezing temperatures, and then wonder why they die not long after we get them home to our sometimes overheated houses.

Here's a tip on how to protect your poinsettia and get it home to your cozy fireside during freezing winter weather. When you go out to shop, take with you a lot of newspaper and a few large rubber bands.

Just before you leave the store, begin wrapping your plant. Find a quiet place where you can lay out half-folded newspaper. Lay one piece over the other in a 6-in. staggered formation so that you have a thick row of paper. Gently lay your plant on its side and begin rolling it up in the staggered sheets. Each sheet will hold its partner down as you continue to roll. Try to cover as much leaf surface as possible. While the pot is on its side, slip a rubber band or two around the pot to hold the newspaper in place. Place the plant(s) in the child's seat of a shopping cart. You'll have room for two poinsettias.

If this plan is too cumbersome for you, you also can use a sturdy brown paper bag. Choose one with handles for carrying and take it with you to the store. If you're going to buy two plants, double-bag them. Set each plant into the sack. This procedure is best done with two people. One puts the bag on the floor and holds it, while the other gathers all the foliage together so that the plants can be placed in the bag without breaking stems or damaging leaves.

I t's no use growing anything in a pot until you realize that the soil is one of your keys to success as a houseplant gardener. Without some sense of soil, your brown thumb syndrome will get worse. Your plants won't live if they are planted in the wrong soil.

What's so important about the soil? The plant sits in it. It's the plant's most immediate environment. From soil, the plant gets water, nourishment, stability (so that it won't topple over), a medium for roots to grow in and easily move through, and maybe a few inches of room to reproduce offsets for the next generation. The soil in its pot is, in fact, home.

You must begin to work with your plants from the ground up, so to speak.

The plant you buy from the garden center will already be potted in the proper soil it requires. You won't have to worry about the growing medium (soil) right away, but you'll have to sooner or later for the following reasons:

• The plant will continue to grow upward and outward. It'll be searching for new root space and, in order to find it, may even send its cramped roots through the drainage hole in the bottom of its pot. And you may take this as a compliment—it's a tribute to your growing skills if your plant has moved this far along in its growth.

• The potting mix will become worn out. As the months pass, the soil becomes less resilient, and the plant will require fresh potting soil from which to draw nutrients to sustain it.

What Do You Know about Soil?

Forget using the soil from your outdoor perennial border. You can't use outdoor garden soil (even if it has been amended) for indoor plants unless you sterilize it in the oven. If you use it straight out of the garden, you'll have a death on your hands. Outdoor soil could have anything in it, and it's too heavy for tropicals and other houseplants.

Roots growing out of drainage holes are a sure sign that it's time to repot.

Different plants require different soils. Finding a good plant-soil match is part of the formula for success. (Photo by Tom Hopkins, New England Stock Photo.)

Sterilizing outdoor garden soil in the oven was much talked about years ago. But those people I've talked to who tried it considered it one of their worst experiments. The problem was that it smelled up the house, and the odor was hard to get rid of. Some inventive die-hards still try to mix up their own soil, but today they use oven cooking bags, which can be sealed to prevent much of the smell from filling the home.

The idea behind the baking process is to destroy harmful organisms, weed seeds, and insect pests that might hurt the plant.

If you still want to bake your own soil, here's how:

1. Put moist (but not wet) soil in a baking pan.

2. Cover it.

3. Bake for 1 hour at 180°F (no higher).

It's believed that even after the soil has been baked, there are sufficient microorganisms in it to help furnish the plant with nutrients, because the organisms continue to break down organic matter in the soil.

A good soil must have the ability to retain moisture, be light enough to ensure good drainage after watering, and be loose enough to allow air to get to plant roots.

The prepackaged potting soils sold on the market today have these character-istics and are (for the most part) good soils, specifically geared to indoor plant culture. Those that actually contain soil are called soil-based potting mixtures, and those without soil are called soilless mixtures. These specific mixes are formulated for all kinds of plants. Here are a few examples:

- **Cacti and succulents.** These plants require a sandy soil that's porous and drains easily.
- **Orchids and bromeliads.** Some bromeliads are epiphytic, which means they live in practically no soil at all, and require an airier medium; others are terrestrial and can be potted in a 30 percent light soil.
- **Azaleas.** These are shallow-rooted plants (there's even a special type of pot called an azalea pot) that like a soil mix with acidic properties and good drainage.
- **African violets.** These plants also need shallow pots and require a light soilless mix with peat moss, perlite, and vermiculite added.
- **Tropical houseplants.** Most of these plants require a light, humusy soil.

What's in Your Potting Soil?

A good potting soil is usually made up of several ingredients. The typical ones are discussed here; later in this chapter, I'll show you how to use these ingredients to make your own potting soil.

Peat moss

Soilless mixes use peat moss as a base for their potting medium. Did you know that the bagged peat moss under your potting bench was composed of the remains of plants? They decayed in boggy (marshy) areas over the centuries and are now farmed as peat moss. But this material has no food value for houseplants—it's used to lighten the potting mix.

The chief value of peat moss is its water-retaining quality. It soaks up water like a sponge and holds it for a long time without making the potting soil a soggy mess. This means that plant roots can get the air they need before the next watering. Peat moss also tends to hold fertilizer longer when it's added to the mix. If peat weren't there, plant fertilizer would leach out of the bottom of the pot via the drainage hole with every watering.

There is one disadvantage to using peat, however. Once it gets dry, it's difficult to remoisten. It forms a hard, dry crust that must be scraped and worked with the fingers before it will reabsorb water. It's best never to let peat moss dry out completely.

When using peat in a potting mix that you make up yourself, it's always a good idea to moisten the peat-based mix just before it goes into the flowerpot. There's a good reason for this. When you put dry peat in the pot around your plant, it's hard to moisten—it keeps wanting to float around in the pot, repelling water. I usually measure out the dry amount I

Five common soil amendments are (clockwise from top left) long-fiber sphagnum moss, peat moss, charcoal, vermiculite, and (center) perlite.

want, and then moisten it as I mix it with the other ingredients and add them to the pot.

Long-fiber sphagnum moss

Sphagnum moss is also a bog moss, but it's used differently. Like peat moss, it's dry when purchased, and you'll find that it has the same water-retentive qualities as peat moss. The advantage is that it's much easier to remoisten once it dries.

Like peat moss, this moss has no food value for plants but keeps the roots moist without being soggy. In fact, it's often used to pot orchids, whose roots must have air around them; and I've used a layer of sphagnum in the bottom of my pots of tropical houseplants to keep their roots damp. I've also used it instead of drainage material for the bottom of pots when I don't have any spare pieces of clay pot about. It keeps the soil in the pot and lets excess water drain out, just as pot shards do.

I recommend that you use sphagnum for double-potting your plants (explained in Chapter 2). This procedure is done to retain moisture or to create a humid condition for plants. And, although there are some people who prefer peat moss for their double-potting, I'm a firm believer that sphagnum works better.

Tree bark

You usually see tree bark in mixes for orchids and bromeliads. These plants must have a light medium (or, in some cases, no medium) around their roots.

Charcoal

Some mixes have charcoal in them, but I'm not talking about the charcoal you use on the outdoor grill. This charcoal can be found in some garden centers and is used to "sweeten" the soil. By this I mean that by adding charcoal to your potting mix, foul odors won't make their presence known—the charcoal absorbs them.

Sometimes you simply must plant in a pot that has no drainage hole. Three good examples of this situation are terrariums, bottle gardens, and pots of spring-flowering bulbs. You know what happens to any excess water (no matter how much) that's left in the bottom of the pot. Before long, the smell begins to overpower the plants or flowers. Some charcoal in the bottom of the pot gets rid of the smell.

I use charcoal two ways: Either I mix a few tablespoons with my potting mix, or I add a thin layer of it in the bottom of the pot. It works well whichever way you choose, and is worth the few cents you pay for a bag of it.

Perlite

Perlite is heat-expanded volcanic rock. Once this excellent product is added to a mix, it helps to keep it aerated. That is, the material prevents the mix from compacting and driving the air out of the soil. Plant roots will get the oxygen they need when perlite is used. In addition, the soil won't stay constantly wet and cause root rot.

As a teenager, I often enjoyed summers by the seaside in Naples, Italy. Several times during the season, the waves washed in volcanic rock, which floated on the surface of the water and was a real snorter to swim through. Perlite is the same kind of stuff, only it's much smaller than the larger floaters that pester swimmers in the Mediterranean.

Vermiculite

Vermiculite is heat-expanded mica and looks like sparkling flakes. This product is often used for rooting cuttings because it holds water and makes an agreeably moist medium for that purpose. I use vermiculite and peat moss together if I have a plant that needs to stay constantly moist but not wet.

Adding charcoal

A bit of charcoal in a pot helps absorb unpleasant odors.

A few of the older houseplant books used to advocate kitty litter as a substitute for vermiculite and perlite in aerating the soil, but I never could understand this. Kitty litter has a clay base. It's absorbent (it has to be for its intended purpose), but it will compact the soil instead of aerating it.

Sand

Sand often is found in potting mixes, but I'm not talking about beach sand here. I mean sharp sand (not fine); it's also called builder's sand or coarse sand (play sand for sandboxes is about the same). It opens up a "tight" soil and allows air to get through to plant roots.

But it also does something else, and this is why I use it. Sand is really good for weighting down a light pot. Have you ever had a plant that was heavier than the pot it was in? This sometimes happens with a blooming amaryllis. The stalk can reach 2 ft. and can topple over a pot because the potting mix for amaryllises is light. How do you solve the problem? Add sand to the mix. Or just add it to the last ½ in. of the pot when planting your bulbs.

There's another reason I like to use sand. It keeps the lighter material in a pot stationary when I water the plant. Have you ever watered a plant only to have the potting material float around in the pot and get on the leaves and flowers? Adding sand to the top ½ in. of the pot will stop this. Don't worry about sand holding water—it doesn't. It allows water to drain right through.

Adding sand to the soil surface

By adding ½ in. of sand to the top of light potting soil you will prevent the plant from tipping over.

Soilless Mixes

Most mixes you see today are soilless; really, they don't contain any soil. Instead, they usually are made up of peat moss, vermiculite, sharp sand, perlite, charcoal, and a small amount of fertilizer.

Always check the list of ingredients on the back of a commercially prepared potting mix to make sure you're buying what your plants need. Not all mixes are created equal. The better mixes are put together scientifically so that there is a proper balance of ingredients for the type of plant being potted.

Why can't I use beach sand in my potting mix?

There are two reasons for this:

- Beach sand has salt in it, which is harmful to plants.
- It's too fine a grain. You need a much coarser (sharper or grittier) grain to lighten soil properly.

Advantages to using soilless mixes

There are a few advantages to soilless mixes, as I've outlined here.

They're light and porous Roots can move through soilless mixes easily, and root growth means top growth. Your plant won't have difficulty increasing in size. The mixes are also porous enough to allow water to drain quickly through the pot's bottom drainage hole. It won't sit in the soil, creating problems like root rot and disease. Plant roots need air, but the only way they get it is by being planted in light potting soil.

They're clean Soilless mixes are easy to handle—they're light and fluffy. They come in plastic bags and are dry; there's no wet mess. The ingredients are clean of any weed seeds and disease organisms.

They're used commercially Plants don't like to have their potting mixes changed at repotting time. They don't like to have to get used to a different kind of soil. Large plants are even more resentful. They often demonstrate how they feel about the matter by refusing to put on any new growth for a while, and may even drop a few leaves to punish you.

Since commercial greenhouses normally use soilless mixes to pot their plants, if you do the same, your plant will have less reason to complain and may begin putting on new growth within a few weeks after you bring it home.

Humans don't like being repotted into new soil either. Moving is a nightmare.

Problems with soilless mixes

There are two problems with today's soilless mixes.

Peat moss The mixes that contain a lot of peat moss are the very devil to water once they go dry in the pot. It takes a while to saturate the peat (scratching the surface of a peat-based mix and flushing the pot with a gallon of water) because the stuff literally repels water. Once it becomes saturated, however, there's no better water-retentive medium.

There is another problem with peat-based mixes: If you allow them to go too dry, they shrink and pull away from the sides of the flowerpot, leaving a small space that allows water to flow right out of the pot as you pour it in. This gives you the impression that the plant has been properly watered when, in fact, the soil around the root ball is still as dry as a bone. You can prevent this by not allowing peat-based mixes to dry out completely, or you can add less peat to the soil mix.

Furthermore, peat-based mixes don't have nutrient value for your plants. Some people add fertilizers to their mix, if they make their own; but later, when the nutrients are either leached out of the pot or used up by the plant, the nutrients must be supplied through a regular schedule of fertilizer feedings.

Weight of the pots Soilless mixes are light. If you're putting a good-sized plant into a plastic pot (which is also light), the pot stands a decent chance of tipping over. There's no bottom weight to keep it upright. In this situation, I always use a clay pot—it's so much heavier than a plastic one. (But I use clay pots for just about everything—I hate plastic. It has no character.)

There *is* something you can do to anchor a light pot, as I mentioned earlier: After you have finished potting your plant, put a ½-in. layer (or more in large pots) of coarse builder's sand on top of the soilless mix.

Potting Soil of the Past

I can remember when the first bags of houseplant potting soil came off the conveyor belts.

It wasn't that good—not at all like the good soilless mixes we have today. I'm talking about the ones developed by the agricultural colleges. Some mixes didn't have perlite or vermiculite added and had very little peat, if any.

I used to buy a small bag of peat and a bag each of perlite and vermiculite. I'd also sneak over to a building site under the cover of darkness (in those days, you could actually set out at night without being attacked) and "procure" a small bucket of coarse builder's sand. Then I'd mix everything together myself.

Because there weren't that many good commercial mixes around, the serious houseplant gardeners I knew had their own favorite recipe for a homemade potting mix. At the time, writers of houseplant books also included their recipes for making the ideal mix; the following is a recipe from an elderly gardener friend. Her plants were always beautiful, and she swore by her mix:

  1 quart topsoil
  1 quart peat moss
  1 quart perlite
  1 quart vermiculite
  1 tablespoon bone meal
  1 handful dry (aged) cow manure
    (no need to be exact)

I tried to duplicate this recipe but never could manage the handful of cow manure. Oddly enough, down through the years I've seen this exact recipe nailed up in different potting sheds, so it must be a good mix.

I'd often thought about ways of solving the problem of the cow manure. I once went so far as to contemplate stopping along the odd country lane. However, this opportunity never presented itself. Country lanes are notorious as places where one might see and not be seen. I always felt as if I were being watched.

Besides, it wasn't the kind of thing I wanted to do in broad daylight. I'd be spotted all right. Spotted and remembered. I even envisioned what the local headlines might scream out at me during a quiet country breakfast:

DAUGHTER OF SOUTHERN BELLE STOOPS LOW

Such tortured thoughts do not a manure thief make. Anyway, with my strong southern sense of right and wrong, I knew I was setting myself up for a lifelong guilt trip. I kept hoping my husband would present me with a few bucketsful of the mellower stuff for Mother's Day—a gift from the heart, so to speak. Fat chance. People who own cows are blessed.

Now that I think back, I remember the potting soil on the market as being a "dark substance," but I'm not sure what it was composed of—the ingredients weren't listed. You had to take the manufacturer's word for it that potting soil was what you were getting. Today, there are no surprises. The ingredients are always listed on the sack, and sometimes the percentage of each component is given.

If the ingredients aren't listed, don't buy the potting soil.

Make Your Own Potting Mix

Some people would rather make their own potting mix (for various reasons), but one reason I make my own is because I think the commercial ones still tend to be a little too heavy or too finely textured. I prefer more sand and peat moss. Everyone has his or her own

Can I crumble up eggshells and add them to my mix for fertilizer?

No. Plants eat with their roots. Anything that's in a liquid state can be taken up by the roots and used. But eggshells aren't liquid. Your plant will have died from old age long before the eggshells have deteriorated sufficiently.

Custom-mixing potting soil

Once you know the soil texture a plant prefers, you can custom-mix its potting soil.

formula for making "the best" potting mix. Here are four recipes I've had luck with.

Recipes 1 and 2

This mix uses a commercial potting mixture but has organic matter (which plants love) added to it for nourishment.

    1 part good commercial potting mix for houseplants
    1 part leaf mold
    1 part builder's sand (not beach sand)

A variation of this recipe is:

    1 part good commercial potting mix for houseplants
    1 part peat moss
    1 part perlite

This is an all-purpose potting mix, good for almost anything except orchids and a few other plants that need to have air

around their roots *all* of the time. Don't worry about being precise on your measurements with the recipes; these aren't exact amounts.

The second recipe is a popular peat-based formula that many of my friends use and is easy to make. They mix up large quantities of it and keep it in big plastic or metal trash cans (with lids) out of the way and in the corner of the garage. Every time they need to repot, the mix is ready for use and is clean.

A word of advice here: Put the container for your made-up mix where you want it, and then mix up the ingredients and put them into the container. Trying to move the container after it's filled is difficult because of the weight of the ingredients, especially the sand.

Many of these friends pour out the ingredients onto a swept garage floor. They use a flat shovel or garden rake to mix things together, then simply fill the trash cans and sweep up what little remains on the floor.

I've used a tarp before, thinking that it would be easy to clean up the area after the mix was in the cans. Wrong. When I tried to get a shovelful of mix, I ended up with a shovelful of tarp. Sweep the floor. This way your children won't walk into the garage with their little friends and catch you swearing.

Recipe 3

Here's another general potting mix:
1 part peat moss
1 part vermiculite (medium grade)
1 part builder's sand

Other friends have told me that they use this recipe but substitute perlite for the sand, thus making the potting mix container much easier to move.

Recipe 4

Here's one last mix that seems to be easier to prepare and more popular among houseplant gardeners than any other. In fact, it's an all-purpose mix that can be used for almost everything.
1 quart builder's sand
1 quart peat moss
1 quart loam
½ handful (no need to be exact) of well-rotted cow manure (if you have compost, you can substitute it for the manure)

TIPS

If you live in an apartment or condominium and can't store your potting mix in large containers, you can make a little of it at a time as you need it. I've had to do this, and it saves room.

I collected all my materials and either took everything out on the balcony or down to the front yard so I could manage any mess and have room to move around. I had a large bucket and trowel (your hand works just as well) for mixing the materials together. I also had a pitcher of warm water in order to slightly moisten the mix before using it to pot a plant. I added the ingredients to the bucket in small batches, keeping everything mixed and moistened as I went. Here are the steps I followed:

1. Add a trowel of each material.
2. Mix.
3. Add a little water.
4. Add another trowel of each material.
5. Mix.
6. Add a little water.

I kept mixing until I had enough to pot my plant. Afterwards, I watered the potted plant and allowed the soil to settle.

The mixing goes fast using this method, and there's little cleanup. If you're working on the balcony, you can use a small tarp—or, better yet, a few sheets of newspaper that can be rolled up and recycled when you're finished.

Before the invention of plastic zipper-locking bags, I used to put any excess mix in old plastic bread bags I had washed out and drip-dried. Now you can put it into reclosable bags. I used to dry out the soil on the balcony *before* bagging it—I didn't want anything nasty growing in the bag. Some plastic bags also have a white label so that you can record the date and what mix the bag contains. Always label everything.

CHAPTER FIVE

HUMIDITY AND VENTILATION

M ost of your houseplants probably originally came from the tropics, where they were used to the high humidity (moisture in the air) of the tropical rain forest. The humidity there stays anywhere from 70 to 90 percent. The humidity also is kept high in commercial greenhouses—to mimic the tropical environment—usually between 75 and 80 percent.

Humidity and Houseplants

"Normal" humidity inside your home may range from 45 to 50 percent. When the central heat comes on in the winter, humidity plummets to 10 to 30 percent—the same percentage of humidity found in desert air. Tropical plants won't survive long under dry conditions like these. Since humidity (and good, light potting soil) is the key to growing tropical houseplants successfully, the *best* percentage to aim at indoors is around 60 percent.

But what actually happens to tropicals in your home if they don't get the humidity they need? Is it all that bad? Judge for yourself. Here are the effects of too little humidity:

• Leaf tips turn brown and shrivel up.
• Leaf edges turn yellow and the leaf wilts.
• Buds on flowers shrivel and fall off.
• Leaves begin to fall off the plant.

And here's something else that'll happen: The wood in your house will shrink, become dry, look lifeless, and lose its character. I'm talking about your wood floors and wood and rattan furniture. Any wood looks better and is in better condition when it has some humidity available.

The general rule of thumb about humidity is this: The higher the temperature is, the greater is the need for humidity.

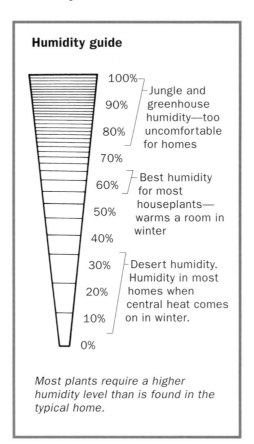

Humidity guide

100% ⌐
90% ⌐ Jungle and greenhouse humidity—too
80% ⌐ uncomfortable for homes
70%
60% ⌐ Best humidity for most houseplants— warms a room in
50% winter
40%
30% ⌐ Desert humidity. Humidity in most
20% homes when central heat comes
10% on in winter.
0%

Most plants require a higher humidity level than is found in the typical home.

When the furnace heat goes on in the winter, the humidity will automatically go down and must be brought back up to a level comfortable for plants. I've stressed trying to duplicate the houseplants' native growing environment; however, raising the humidity in your home to 75 percent will cause you to keel over. But there are solutions to the problem of humidity that you can use to make life bearable for both you and your plants.

How to raise the humidity in your home

Here are a few solutions for creating a microclimate around your plants and raising the humidity to 50 or 60 percent in *their area alone.* The rest of the house will not be affected by the elevated humidity to the point of discomfort, but you will breathe better and your wood furniture will look less brittle and washed out.

Pebble trays *Grouped plants* Use pebble trays to raise the humidity around your plants. Group all of your plants that need high humidity—*leave cacti and succulents out.* Determine how many tropicals you have. If your plant collection is large, find a sheet-metal specialist who can make you a shallow, waterproof, metal tray (about 4 in. deep). If you want it to cover a large area, it should sit on the floor. Ask the metalworker to be sure the tray is watertight—you don't want to ruin your carpet or wood floor. You may even prefer to line the tray with a thick sheet of plastic (clear plastic is not too noticeable) as an added precaution.

Much smaller trays can be bought ready-made from garden centers. I also have seen gardeners use a large, neutral color, heavy-duty kitty-litter tray—you see different sizes in grocery and pet stores. These are made of plastic and don't require a lining.

Next, purchase pea gravel (try a pet store or look in the pet section of a

Grouped plants in a pebble tray

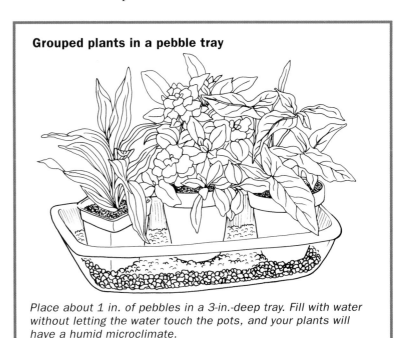

Place about 1 in. of pebbles in a 3-in.-deep tray. Fill with water without letting the water touch the pots, and your plants will have a humid microclimate.

Red-margined dracaena (Dracaena marginata) is one of the many humidity lovers. (Photo by Janet Loughrey.)

grocery or department store) or pebbles. Line the tray with 1 in. or 1½ in. of gravel; then set all of your tropical houseplants on it. Make sure you put saucers under them—plant roots love the moist growing conditions of the pebble tray and will try to grow into it.

When you water the plants, any excess water will flow out into the gravel. The plants remain high and dry *above* the water. But the best part is that you've created a microclimate around your plants. The evaporation of the water around your plants provides the needed humidity in their area alone.

Individual plants   You can go to the garden center, find deeper saucers, and make up individual pebble trays for each potted plant. Fill each saucer with small pebbles, add a little warm water, and set your plants on the pebbles out of the water.

I have some objections, however, to these individual trays:

- The tray surface is so small for each plant that you have to wonder just how much humidity each receives.
- This method may work well for small plant collections, but larger collections can't be accommodated by individual saucers with pebbles. It's far more efficient and cost effective if several large pebble trays are made and used.

- Then, too, you're in constant fear of the dog upsetting all the small trays and plants so that you have a domino effect of falling plants and pebbles, and water everywhere.

If you like the individual tray idea but don't like the pebbles, try this twist. Use a block of wood to elevate the pot above the water in the saucer. After watering your plants, just let the excess water stay in the saucers and allow it to humidify. This method seems more practical.

Electric humidifiers   You can try using humidifiers. I'm talking about the small electric humidifiers you see for sale in drugstores—the ones used in a child's sickroom. This is the type of humidifier I talked about in Chapter 3. They're inexpensive, and they're perfect for setting up a microclimate around the *immediate area* of your plants.

A little portable humidifier will come in handy during the winter months when the furnace heat is turned on. Furnace heat dries air out as it heats up your home, but a humidifier replaces the moisture in the air and actually raises the temperature in your home several degrees (this is another reason why I love electric humidifiers—I hate to pay heating bills).

If you can keep the humidity in your home at 50 percent in the winter, you can lower your thermostat nearly 6°F and *still* feel just as warm. Humidity warms the air. Just ask southern gardeners who work outdoors in muggy summer weather—they'll tell you that 75°F feels like 85° if the humidity is up. Plants love this because they can maintain the cool temperatures they like in the winter during their dormancy period and still have their humidity.

Electric humidifiers are an effective and generally inexpensive way to give plants the humidity level they need. And that's good for you, too.

I keep a little humidifier going in the plant room from late fall (when the furnace kicks in) throughout the winter—you wouldn't believe the effect on the plants. Not only is the air moist and warm, but the foliage is thick and lush. Larger leaf surface means the plant takes in more sunlight for growth. By spring, everything looks bigger (even though the plants are in their resting mode) and healthier.

There's one more thing the humidifier does—it prevents spider mites (the number one pest of houseplants) from setting up shop among your plants. They *hate* humidity (more about this pest in Chapter 8).

Misters   There are misters specifically made for use on plants, but only a few will last you over the years. What you want is something that will hold a quantity of warm water so that you don't wear out the carpet as you constantly run back for refills. In the 1970s, I remember the little glass and brass misters on the market (misting was *it* then) "specially designed for indoor plants." They worked well—if you only had one plant (or if your residence was Lilliput). They held about a cup of water. Twenty or 30 plants would have sent you to the emergency room (we didn't have such ailments as carpal tunnel syndrome in those days; we had sore wrists).

Misting is supposed to be beneficial because it removes dirt and dust from plant leaves. It also discourages spider mites by leaving a fine mist of water over your plants and raising the humidity. This is all very nice for those who are mist-minded; but in my experience, other things get misted besides the plants. And all too soon that mist evaporates (especially on hot days in the

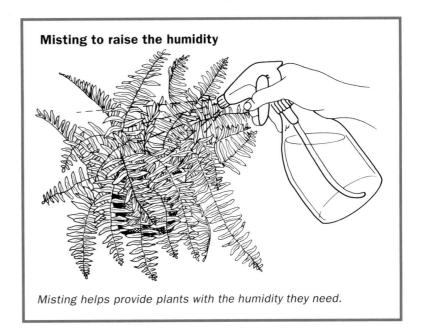

Misting to raise the humidity

Misting helps provide plants with the humidity they need.

summer, or in furnace-heated air), and the plants are just as deprived of humidity as before.

I've seen dedicated gardeners mist themselves silly in an effort to keep their tropicals humidified. During the 1960s houseplant craze, the idea of a steam vapor humidifier hadn't been talked about as an addition to the home houseplant area. But we have them now, so I don't mist at all. One young woman I know was late for her wedding because of detailed misting instructions she felt duty-bound to impart to her house sitter.

Double-potting   Double-potting keeps a plant cool and evenly moist. It also raises the humidity around the plant. See Chapter 2 for detailed instructions.

The shower   Put your tropical plants in the bathtub, close the curtain, and spray them with warm water from the shower (don't do this to cacti and succulents). Besides raising the humidity, you'll also be watering, washing their leaves, and discouraging spider mites—four birds

Outside, plants can take advantage of naturally higher humidity levels. (Photo by Karen Bussolini.)

The tips of the leaves
of my ferns turn
brown, die, and fall off
during the winter. Is
this a humidity
problem?

Yes. When the water rises
faster into the leaves
than it can be replaced by
the roots, the leaves farthest from the roots turn
brown and die.

You undergo a similar
process (although your
body parts don't fall off).
In winter when the fur-
nace heat is turned on,
your nose and throat be-
come sore or dry, espe-
cially upon waking in the
morning. The mucous
membranes are usually lu-
bricated, but warm, dry
air dries them out. You
could benefit from a hu-
midifier in your home. An
hour or so in a room with
increased humidity will
put you and your plants
right once again.

with one stone! After the plants have been thoroughly soaked, leave them to sit in the humid tub for a few hours while they drain. They'll love it.

Mother Nature In the spring when the weather's warm, set your plants outside. Let the rainfall water, feed, and humidify them. I do this every year. Most of my plants vacation outdoors from May until October 1 (it's *still* hot in Tennessee in October). They stay in a sheltered area, which allows them just the amount of light they need and lets them take advantage of the nitrogen-rich rainfall. Besides, by spring I'm tired of tending them and would rather turn them over to Mother for a few months—she's done this kind of thing before.

Groupings You may not know it, but a plant generates its own humidity. Water rises from the roots and flows into the leaves where it's given off as water vapor around the plant's immediate vicinity. So if the humidity is too low in the air around the plant, water is drawn up from the roots and sent to the leaves to solve the problem.

Use this principle to provide your houseplants with needed humidity. Group all the tropicals together near your light source and allow them to humidify each other. But be sure to allow for air circulation *between* the plants. You don't want them sharing fungi and diseases too.

How do I handle humidity problems? I put most of my plants outside in a sheltered area for the spring and summer and let nature tend them, and when the furnace comes on in the winter, I use an inexpensive electric humidifier. I camouflage it so that it can't easily be seen by visitors but is easy to refill with water when necessary.

Puddles If it's summer and hot either on your back patio where you've placed your plants in a sheltered area or in your greenhouse, you have the ideal means of increasing the humidity that can't be used indoors. On the patio, spritz your foliage with a misting spray and make puddles on the patio around your plants. It'll be humid all day long. In the greenhouse, keep the floor damp or leave puddles there after you've spritzed plants. In both places, it's also important to allow breezes or air to circulate about the area, because you don't want *still* heat and humidity; this causes rot. You want humidity with circulating air—always.

Don't forget that your outdoor and greenhouse hanging plants also need humidity. They, too, should benefit from being hung over puddles outdoors or over the wet greenhouse floor. Some gardeners advocate the use of drip saucers (filled with water and suspended under the hanging basket) to provide the needed humidity. They think this will sufficiently humidify a basket plant. Sure it will—for about 20 minutes on a hot day. These people don't live in the South or out West; they have no idea what an inferno it can become in high summer. What are we expected to do, then? Run back and forth with cups of water, refilling all the suspended saucers underneath all of our baskets? The idea is to enjoy houseplants, not become a slave to them.

These same people advocate that we hang all of our basket plants close together so that they can share the humidity they each give off through transpiration. Fine. But the rules on the ground also apply to the air. Just as you shouldn't group all of your plants close together on the ground or floor, don't hang your plants close together. More than just humidity will be shared. I'm talking rot—"And, it sher ain't purdy," as an elderly Texan gardener once told me. So, hang 'em high, but don't hang 'em close.

Too much humidity

Can you ever get too much humidity? It can happen. Excessive humidity can cause fungus diseases. Humidity is essential to plants, and they grow better in it, but too much of a good thing . . . you get the idea.

Think about it for a minute. Things that disintegrate easily, such as wood, don't last very long in humid jungles. There's an old story about doctor-philosopher Albert Schweitzer that I think is appropriate here. He was a first-rate pianist, and when he went to Africa to begin his life's missionary work among the native peoples, he took his piano—a wooden piano. It lasted only a few months. The high humidity of the jungle rotted the wood. He did replace that piano with a metal one.

So, what can happen to plants if too much humidity is provided?
- Mold spots form on the leaves.
- Dark spots appear on leaves and stems; these are rot spots.
- The flowers look moldy.

Remember, not all plants need high humidity. And if you supply it to those that don't need it, you'll be letting your plants in for fungus problems—and eventual death. In botanical greenhouses, the cacti and succulents are always kept away from the tropicals because they don't need the high humidity that the tropicals do.

Know your plants.

Houseplants that require high humidity

Most houseplants will take average household humidity of 45 to 50 percent. But the following plants need much more. They're used to 65 or 75 percent, and they'll grow better if they get it. Unfortunately, high humidity like this is uncomfortable for people.

You can grow these plants off to themselves in an area you don't usually frequent. The humidity in that area can easily be brought up to 60 percent if you use a combination of the methods described earlier in this chapter. If the decision were mine, I'd use an electric humidifier, because it's all you need to get the humidity up to an acceptable level.

- Aluminum plant (*Pilea cadierei*)
- Baby's tears (*Soleirolia soleirolii*)
- Bird's-nest fern (*Asplenium nidus*)
- Boston fern (*Nephrolepis exaltata* 'Bostoniensis')
- Corn plant (*Dracaena fragrans* 'Massangeana')
- Delta maidenhair (*Adiantum raddianum*)
- Flame violet (*Episcia cupreata*)
- Florist's cyclamen (*Cyclamen persicum*)
- Gold-dust dracaena (*Dracaena surculosa*)
- Goldfish plant (*Columnea × banksii* and *C. gloriosa*)
- Peacock plant (*Calathea makoyana*)
- Pigtail anthurium (*Anthurium scherzeranum*)
- Rabbit's foot fern (*Davallia fejeensis*)
- Red-margined dracaena (*Dracaena marginata*)
- Rex begonia (*Begonia × rex-cultorum*)
- Ti plant (*Cordyline terminalis*)
- Trailing watermelon begonia (*Pellionia daveauana*)
- Wandering Jew (*Zebrina pendula*)
- Zebra plant (*Aphelandra squarrosa*)

I have a room where I grow plants under artificial light. The problem is that the temperature stays in the high 80s in the room because of the lights. Plant growth is weak. Is the heat affecting plant growth?

Yes. Try these solutions:

- Vent the room first. You must get air circulating; open the windows.

- Try using an exhaust fan in an open window. This will take the hot air out of the room. Greenhouses use this method; their fans are set to go on when the temperature reaches 75°F.

- Put a small electric humidifier in the room to raise the humidity (you can keep it on a timer for convenience).

- Install a small air-conditioner away from the plants.

Signs of too much humidity

With high humidity and low air circulation, look for moldy leaves and flowers and rotting leaves and stems.

Ventilation for Houseplants

Ventilation and air circulation are a part of houseplant culture that is often overlooked. But plants need fresh air for the same reasons we do. Yes, they can live in terrariums for years, but even terrarium hobbyists recommend fresh air for their enclosed plants every now and then. Just like us, plants don't like stuffy, overheated, or freshly painted rooms.

Houseplants want air flowing over and under their leaves, and some plants need it more than others. Remember, the success of the green thumb gardener is to try to approximate the plant's native environment.

Do you have any of the plants listed below? They need good ventilation and air circulating around them, or they'll easily begin turning yellow, losing leaves, and rotting:

- Bay or sweet bay *(Laurus nobilis)*
- Cacti
- Calamondin (× *Citrofortunella mitis)*
- Castor-oil plant *(Ricinus communis)*
- Dwarf pomegranate (*Punica granatum* 'Nana')
- Geraniums (*Pelargonium* species)
- Impatiens (*Impatiens* species)
- Norfolk Island pine *(Araucaria heterophylla)*
- Orchids
- Passionflower (*Passiflora* species)
- Piggyback plant *(Tolmiea menziesii)*
- Poor man's orchid or butterfly flower *(Schizanthus)*
- Primrose jasmine *(Jasminum mesnyi)* or pink jasmine *(J. polyanthum)*
- Spineless yucca *(Yucca elephantipes)*
- Succulents

What fresh air does for houseplants

Air temperature If plants are in a hot room during the summer, fresh air will *lower* the air temperature around them. Houseplants don't like high temperatures; 70°F suits them just fine, and 85°F puts them into stress. But 85°F with lots of fresh air streaming in through the window is better than a closed room at 85°F. Keeping your plants outdoors in the summer under sheltered areas also will ensure that they get the breezes they need.

Humidity Fresh air will *lower* the humidity in an overcrowded area that stays warm and moist all the time. Remember the jungle? Things rot fast in moist, hot, still conditions. And even though your home is far from being a jungle, your houseplants still can get fungus diseases—which can spread. I've seen whole plant collections thrown out because fungus disease was able to take hold and spread from plant to plant.

Fresh air should be allowed to circulate around your plants, especially if you use the grouping method for plants like tropicals. Don't place your houseplants so close together that they appear bunched. Spread them apart so that air can get in among leaves and branches.

Odors Fresh air removes foul odors from an enclosed area. Houseplants are in damp soil, which, naturally, has an odor. They're always dropping leaves and other pieces of themselves onto the soil, where these things may stay until they rot. After a while, in a closed space, it all starts smelling a little strong.

This is not to say that houseplants don't have their sweet fragrances—they do. I love the heady, fresh smell of chlorophyll that fills the air around Swedish ivy. It's a sweet perfume to me and is even more evident if the temperature of the room is 65°F and there's a window open. The plant is a natural air freshener. But the decomposing process that takes place in a damp pot is *always* there and is not pleasant. Bacteria work to break down rotting plant material, and the whole business can get smelly when you have a stuffy room full of plants.

Ways to provide ventilation

Providing ventilation is not as difficult for the houseplant gardener as providing light to a dim area. These strategies are simple, although a few could mean a little investment.

• **Open windows.** This is the easiest way, especially if you have two windows in the room, which will give you a cooling cross breeze. But if the temperature outside is a lot less than that in your plant room, don't open a window. Doing so will let in cold drafts, and plants hate them. Your plants may show you just how much by voicing their opinion of what you've done.

Wait until the outdoor and indoor temps are comfortable—then open your room to the outdoors.

• **Circulate the air in the room with a small fan.** Fans come in all sizes. Choose from free-standing, table, and floor models. The smaller ones are not expensive and will last for years with proper cleaning. At the end of the season, I take the grill off mine (some are detachable) and remove the fan blades. Then I wash grill and blades carefully in warm, soapy water, rinsing and drying before putting them back together. I store the fans clean, so they'll be ready for the next season.

• **Use an exhaust fan in an open window.** These are fans that take the hot room air and blow it out the window. Greenhouses use something like this method. Their fans are set by thermostat to go on when the temperature reaches 75°F. These fans

Aloe (*Aloe vera*) is accustomed to high temperatures and low humidity, so give it good air circulation. (Photo by Jim Schwabel, New England Stock Photo.)

A shot of color within the stark landscape of winter makes growing houseplants worthwhile. (Photo by Derek Fell.)

are a must in large greenhouses where the glass or plastic amplifies the heat and light.

• **Install a small air-conditioner.** These are fine for circulating air in a stuffy or hot room. Don't try to solve your ventilation problems by setting your houseplant collection near an air-conditioner, though. Plants don't care for blasts of cold or heat.

In spring and fall, open your windows and let in the air. Plants are used to it in their own native environments—why not in yours? Many people (myself included) summer their plants outdoors in sheltered areas out of direct sun, wind, and downpours. Plants come back inside in the fall looking revitalized and ready to enter their dormancy cycle, invigorated and healthy. By that time, you're ready to have them inside with you again because things are winding down at the end of the growing season outside. A room filled with green plants in the dead of winter cheers the heart.

CHAPTER SIX

FOOD

Normally, Mother Nature would provide some kind of food for your plants if they were in their native environment. Dead and decaying organic material would break down and sooner or later be incorporated into the soil around the plant. Water from rains would carry liquefied material farther into the soil, where it would be taken up as food by the plant. That's how Mother works with her garden.

But when you're stuck in a pot and can't get out or at least let your roots run around in search of goodies, then you're a captive. Things have to be done for you and to you—you can't go in search of them yourself.

You may be wondering why it's necessary to feed plants at all. Doesn't the soil in the flower pot contain all that the plant needs to grow? For a short time, yes. The new potting mix you bought to repot your houseplants into will have some food value for about two months. But that's it, and here's why. Each time you water the plant, a little food is taken up by the roots for use in cell repair, growth, and flower production. But some of it is also washed out of the pot with the water as it seeps from the drainage hole. This process is called "leaching."

By the end of two months, there isn't any food left in the small space of a pot to feed the plant—it's been leached out.

It must be replaced, and this is where you come in. You'll need to begin applying a type of plant food.

Plant Food:
Types and Methods of Use

There are two principal types of plant food: water soluble and time release. But there are many ways you can administer the fertilizer to your houseplants, and some work better than others.

Signs of not enough food

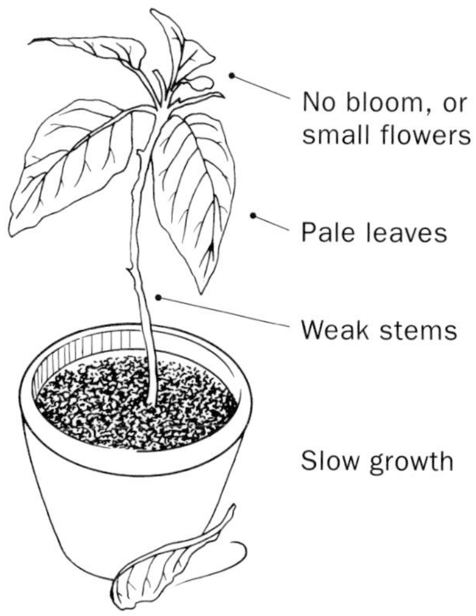

No bloom, or small flowers

Pale leaves

Weak stems

Slow growth

Without enough food, plants develop weak stems, have yellow or pale leaves, and often drop their lower leaves.

What happens if your plant doesn't get the fertilizer it needs?

- Growth is slow.
- The plant has little resistance to pests and diseases.
- The leaves look pale and may have yellow spots.
- The flowers are of poor quality, if they appear at all.
- The stem is weak.
- The lower leaves drop.

Liquid, granular, stick, and powder fertilizers make feeding your plants precise and convenient.

It comes in small containers, mixes quickly in water, and is sprayed on or watered in.

Following the manufacturer's instructions on the side of the container, you mix a measured amount of the food into warm water. There is usually a little measuring scoop for powders and an eyedropper or measuring cup for liquids included in the package. Then you use the liquid to water your plants.

Water-soluble plant food is the best way to fertilize because plants can use food only if it's in a liquid state. They don't eat anything solid. That's why crumbling up eggshells and sprinkling them in the pot or adding them to the potting soil doesn't work.

The following are the most common methods of administering water-soluble fertilizer.

Water-soluble fertilizer

Water-soluble plant food comes in powder and liquid forms. You've seen this kind of plant food advertised each spring and summer in TV commercials.

Constant-feed method Constant-feed fertilizing is the easiest approach. With this fertilizing technique, you bring a low dose of water-soluble food to your plant every time you water. You won't be tied to a feeding regimen or wonder when you last fed the plants. Was it last week or only Monday?

When you feed with a water-soluble plant food, use it at one-quarter the recommended strength in warm water. Manufacturers inflate the nutrient needs of potted plants, which don't really require as much food as the directions call for. And there is always a chance of overfertilization, as well as a buildup of fertilizer salts, which can harm plants.

It's so easy to overfertilize houseplants. Beginners think that a little more food than is recommended will make the plant even larger and healthier. Unfortunately, the opposite is true. The plant takes only what it needs, and the rest of the fertilizer sits in the soil and accumulates as fertilizer salts.

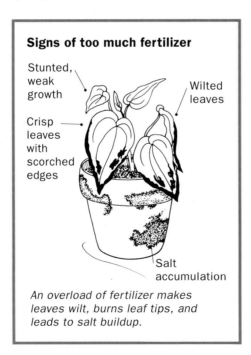

Signs of too much fertilizer

Stunted, weak growth

Wilted leaves

Crisp leaves with scorched edges

Salt accumulation

An overload of fertilizer makes leaves wilt, burns leaf tips, and leads to salt buildup.

Overfertilization also can cause other problems. Leaves will look burned at their tips; the leaf tip turns brown and dries out like paper—this is dead tissue. You've probably seen the result of people trying to repair damaged leaf tips by using a pair of scissors to cut off the burned part. But the damage just comes back, and the leaves end up looking artificial and tinkered with. The brown color is a result of root damage. Many times, what we do to the plant (such as underwatering, overwatering, and overfertilization) shows up in the roots first and then in the leaves.

Using water-soluble plant food via the constant-feed method means that there is no feast-or-famine syndrome—just a nice, even feeding schedule. Applications of fertilizer are usually made (according to the package instructions) on a continual basis when you water your plants.

Here's why the constant-feed method is best for your plants: A plant that's fed only once a month feasts for a week and then goes hungry for the rest of the month until the next month's fertilizer is

applied. This is because each time you water the plant, more food leaches out through the bottom drainage hole until there isn't any left. You don't eat this way. It's better for the plant if a small amount of fertilizer (a prescribed amount according to package instructions) is given on a regular basis rather than every now and then.

Foliar-feeding method Foliar feeding also uses water-soluble fertilizer. This method allows plants to take in nutrients through their leaves rather than through their roots. The food is mixed with water and sprayed on the plant's leaves, which absorb the liquid.

I remember when foliar feeding was first recognized in houseplant literature. The method was widely used when the bromeliad craze first hit. People discovered that bromeliads could take moisture out of the air and absorb it through their leaves, so they began to feed *all* of their plants by misting the leaves with a water-soluble food.

The leaves on the left, from a citrus plant, show signs of chlorosis, an iron deficiency. The leaves on the right are from a healthy citrus plant.

What happens if my plant gets too much fertilizer?

- The leaves wilt
- Fertilizer salts appear on the surface of the potting soil
- Summer growth is not robust
- Winter growth is weak and thin
- Leaves look burned on their edges and tips

Foliar-feed your bromeliads

Bromeliads are good candidates for foliar feeding, since they readily absorb nutrients through their leaves.

Is salt buildup normal?

Yes. All houseplants get it at one time or another. If nutrients aren't taken in by your plants, they just sit around and accumulate. The fertilizer can build up to the point that the roots are damaged. Burned roots will show up in burned leaves.

Some garden writers then pooh-poohed the idea and called it a fad. They felt that bromeliads (which are epiphytic plants) are specially adapted to take moisture and nutrients through their leaves but that other plants aren't. Some gardeners believed that a little mist feeding here and there wouldn't do much to help houseplants anyway.

Today, foliar feeding is a widely accepted method of getting food into plants—and it's big business. TV commercials appear early every spring, showing people watering their perennial borders with foliar food. A lot of companies have jumped on the bandwagon and have even constructed their own special watering containers, which they sell along with their fertilizer. You've seen these packaged deals each spring at the local supermarkets and department stores.

What the people in the TV commercial don't tell you is that the effects of foliar feeding last only two weeks. Then foliar feeding has to be repeated if the plant is to get regularly scheduled feedings. Foliar feeding is like getting a vitamin B_{12} shot.

It's a quick fix—it gives you energy and makes you feel great just after you've had it, but it has no long-term effect. Needless to say, plants can get pretty hungry between foliar feedings.

I also should add that a fertilizer with chelated iron (which is used for plants suffering from chlorosis—a nutrient disorder) works well if it's sprayed on the foliage. I've used this method often on both indoor and outdoor plants. Chlorosis is much like iron-deficiency anemia in humans. Leaves appear pale or even yellow, although the veins of the leaves remain dark green. But, once again, this application is only a bandage. It won't fix the problem of malnourished plants, and the chlorosis will return. Repotting into a good, nutrient-packed potting mix is usually what's needed.

Time-release fertilizer

There are two methods for feeding plants with time-release fertilizer: surface and root feeding. Fertilizer for the surface method is available as granules; for the root-feeding method, tablets or sticks can be used.

Surface method The granular type of fertilizer is scattered on top of the soil (instructions are on the package container) and then watered in. As the water flows over the granules, a small amount of fertilizer seeps into the soil and is carried to the roots. After applying this granular food once, you don't have to reapply it again for three or more months.

You may already have this fertilizer in some of your pots without knowing it. Have you visited a garden center recently and bought a plant? Look into the pot. Do you see tiny balls or pellets lying on top? That's the time-release fertilizer. Growers add it to pots before the plants

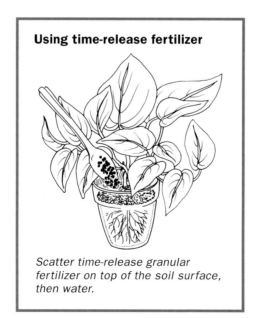

Using time-release fertilizer

Scatter time-release granular fertilizer on top of the soil surface, then water.

are shipped for purchase because it's easier for them to feed their plants this way. They can't use water-soluble plant food because it's too time-consuming. They have thousands of plants to feed.

And you may not want to use a water-soluble food if you're on the go constantly, catching trains and planes. If this is the way your life is ordered, time-release fertilizer was made for you. You don't have to take time out of your busy schedule to measure water-soluble feedings for each of your plants. You just measure one feeding for all of your plants, and you're set for three months. All you have to remember is to water. Plant sitters taking care of your plants while you're away won't have to fertilize, either. The food already will be there.

Miss Julia, an elderly gardener friend, knew she had to have surgery and that she'd be unable to carry out her regular fertilizer program after she returned home from the hospital. She added time-release fertilizer to all her plants before going to the hospital, and her plant sitter simply watered her plants while she was away. The time-release fertilizer fed each plant every time it was watered, and Miss Julia was greeted on her return by pots full of healthy growth.

Another friend, Brooks, uses this method of feeding only part of the year. During the summer, he writes and has time to personally see to his plants, so he uses water-soluble food. In the fall, he returns to his usual hectic job and switches to a time-release feeding, which he applies every three months.

But, in spite of the many advantages to using time-release fertilizer, there are a couple of drawbacks. Continual use will guarantee that fertilizer salts will build up on top of the soil, creating problems for your plants (more about this later). And,

like most things created for our convenience, this food costs a lot more than water-soluble food.

Root-feeding method The tablet and stick forms of time-release fertilizer are meant to be stuck down into the soil. Then, when you water, they're supposed to release fertilizer to the root zone of the plant.

I don't use tablets or sticks. I don't think they do a good job of spreading themselves around. They seem to me to be a bit concentrated in one spot only. And then there's always the problem of control: How do you get them to stop adding fertilizer to the soil when the plant's dormant cycle comes around and you must withhold fertilizers?

In talking to other houseplant gardeners, I've found that one's choice of fertilizer is about as personal as his or her

Using stick fertilizers

Stick fertilizer

Make sure stick fertilizers are placed in the plant's root zone, so the roots can take up the nutrients.

MAIN PLANT NUTRIENTS	
Nutrient	What It Does
Nitrogen (N)	Gives leaves their green color and promotes overall growth
Phosphorus (P)	Develops flower buds and root growth
Potassium (K) or potash	Develops strong stems and resistance to disease

How do I know what nutrients my plants need?

- If flower buds are setting, use a high-phosphorus, low-nitrogen mix to encourage bloom.

- If foliage is pale or yellow, use a high-nitrogen mix.

- If you're growing seedlings, use a mild, high-phosphorus mix made specifically for transplants.

choice of underwear. Some wouldn't use a product if you gave it to them. Others swear by that same product and will use it for decades.

What's in Plant Food?

There are three main nutrients that plants need: nitrogen, phosphorus, and potassium. The nutrients are abbreviated by chemists as N, P, and K, respectively. Fertilizer manufacturers often simply use these letters on their packaging, and sometimes they use only numbers. For example, a formulation reading 5-10-5 contains 5 percent nitrogen, 10 percent phosphorus, and 5 percent potassium. Houseplant food has some or all of these nutrients and also may have secondary nutrients (sulfur, calcium, and magnesium) and trace elements (boron, copper, iron, molybdenum, zinc, manganese, and chlorine), depending on the manufacturer.

Since each family of plants is different, the percentages of each nutrient differ, depending upon the needs of that particular family. For example, African violet plant food is formulated differently from bromeliad food. The above chart explains what each main nutrient does and provides tips on which fertilizers fit your plants best.

Here are some common NPK percentages:

- **20-20-20:** General, all-purpose food (for the entire plant)

- **30-10-10:** Houseplant food (high-nitrogen mix stimulates leaf growth)
- **12-36-14:** African violet food (high-phosphorus mix stimulates bloom)
- **5-1-1:** Fish fertilizer (mild, for tropicals and older plants)

Houseplant folklore says: Apply fertilizer when the plant grows a new leaf. Well, things move a little faster around my house now, and I often don't notice when a plant grows a new leaf. So I decided to stay with the constant-feed method and use water-soluble fertilizer given at one-quarter the package-recommended strength. This way, I won't overfertilize my plants, and fertilizer salt stands less chance of accumulating.

In the 1970s, I saw the first acid-type fertilizer for plants that prefer growing in acidic soil. Evidently, someone realized that gardenias, camellias, and azaleas needed it. Now, acid-type fertilizer is everywhere, and everyone uses it.

In the past, there were a few houseplant authorities who advocated making your own liquid concoction and using it as plant food. They suggested that you collect eggshells, lettuce leaves, vegetable peelings and parings and then throw them all into a blender (there weren't any food processors then). You were to liquefy everything; and to this liquefied stuff, you were to add a little water. You were then supposed to pour this slurry onto the soil as fertilizer for your houseplants.

You organic gardeners will recognize this technique as a variation of composting—the material is just liquefied instead of chopped, and then added to the soil.

I do something similar when I take a pail of kitchen waste out to the vegetable garden. I dig a hole in the center of the bed where four tomato plants have been planted, throw the kitchen waste in, and cover the hole. Earthworms flock to the area, eat the garbage, and pay me back by fertilizing the soil with their nitrogen-rich castings. The tomatoes planted around the hole go crazy; they grow out of their 6-ft. cages and put on plump, red tomatoes in no time. Now, that's what I call working with nature.

But when you pour this liquefied material onto soil that's contained in a pot, and wait a few days, you're asking for the kind of smell that causes a high-school chemistry class to evacuate the building. Whoever wrote about doing this didn't try it. The method does work—don't get me wrong. But you have to dig a hole, dump the stuff, then cover it up. Leaving the foul mess to lie on the surface of the soil is just asking for it—from the family dog, ants, toddlers, microorganisms, and anything that lives off decaying matter. It's probably best not to use liquid compost on your houseplants.

How to Fertilize

Always follow the printed instructions on the packaged fertilizer product you buy, but cut the strength to one-quarter. Potted plants don't need that much food, and what they don't use will just sit on the soil as fertilizer salts.

Some houseplant gardeners set aside one week in the month when they don't fertilize at all. I do this and recommend it. Use warm water *alone* to water your

The accumulation of fertilizer salts creates this white, chalky buildup on pots.

plants, and water thoroughly. By *thoroughly,* I mean flush all pots with water several times and let the water drain through the drainage hole quickly. The reason for doing this is that fertilizer salts accumulate on top of the soil and on the sides of the pot. These salts will eat into the stem of a plant or leaf that touches them—that's how caustic they really are. By flushing your pots every now and then, hopefully the salts will be leached out of the pot instead of accumulating on the soil. You'll eventually get those ugly accumulations of salt, but flushing will forestall their appearance.

These salts can even accumulate on the rims of plastic pots. Yes, they can be cleaned off, but it often requires some scrubbing on your part. Later in this chapter I'll tell you how to clean pots that have accumulated fertilizer salt buildup.

Fertilizing an old friend

We've all had those monster plants that we've kept over the years. Whenever you've pulled up stakes and moved, they've gone with you. They were present when your firstborn child was brought

What causes fertilizer salt buildup?

Several things cause fertilizer salt buildup, and some of those things aren't from fertilizers—they may be from your water. Eventually, all pots will show a buildup of white crusty stuff on the surface of the pot and/or the soil. Here's what causes it:

- Watering plants too often from the bottom
- Overfertilizing or feeding too often
- Using time-release fertilizers for several years
- Keeping the plant too long in the same pot

home from the hospital, and they're still around when he or she goes off to college. Throughout the years and after numerous repottings, they've exceeded all expectations in growth and have reached the limit for indoor comfort. These are the old fellows you've grown up with. You don't want them to get any bigger or you'll be forced to get rid of an old friend. Yet you need to feed them to keep them looking lush and vibrant. What do you do?

You do what we all have to do when we've been around for a long time—eat less, but eat well. This means fewer feedings of a dilute, good-quality fertilizer. It also means that the plant won't be repotted anymore because it's far too big to be moved. From now on, instead of repotting, topdressing with good soil will be necessary (more about topdressing in Chapter 7).

When you feed your monster plant, use a water-soluble fertilizer at one-quarter the manufacturer's recommended strength and mix it in warm water. Apply this feeding solution only a few times during the year. I give two feedings—the first in early spring (March), and the second in high summer (July). Your purpose in decreased feedings is to give the plant what it needs to sustain its health but not enough to continue its growth. Doing this will ensure a continued relationship for years to come.

When to Fertilize

The growth cycle for most houseplants follows a predictable pattern. Early spring is when they begin to grow, and fall is when they begin to rest (go dormant). of This cycle is geared chiefly to the length of daylight hours, but temperature also plays a part.

It makes sense, therefore, that most plants should be fed only when they're actively growing, since that's the only time they can use the food. If they aren't growing and making new tissue, why feed them at all?

Now, look (you may say), the plants are indoors where the temperature is comfortable, and they're given all the light and warmth they need, so why not feed them? Because you can't fool them. They still know when it's time to wind down for the year, and they'll do it in spite of your efforts to keep them going full steam all year long—it's in their genetic makeup. If you've ever noticed, all living things have a wind-down cycle so that a period of rest can take place.

This rest is necessary for normal cell repair and growth. Humans require a dormant or rest cycle every day, and it's triggered by light, although other factors are involved. Plants go through a brief rest at night, too—they don't absorb much in the way of nutrients. But the longer dormant cycle that plants go through takes place in winter.

Plants begin entering their dormancy in the fall—starting in September. Fewer leaves are produced, and flowering is over for the year. Some outdoor plants even start shedding the year's growth (after first turning lovely colors) by dropping leaves to signal that their rest cycle has begun. During the winter months, most houseplants rest completely. They require very little in the way of warmth, food, or water (but they *still* need good light, air circulation, and humidity). Then, in the early spring (about late February or March), they begin waking up. At this time they want what you'd want— warmth, food, and water. Watch your plants closely during these early spring months. The addition of any new growth

Is there anything I can do to get rid of salts on the soil?

Yes. Scrape the surface of the soil, loosen the salts, and throw the stuff away. You can add some good houseplant potting mix to fill in the space.

Remember: Houseplants don't need much food. What they don't take in just sits there, creating a fertilizer salt buildup problem.

signals that the plant is ready to begin its growth cycle for the new year.

How should you handle a plant's dormant cycle? It's best *not* to feed any plant that's getting ready to go into dormancy. I never feed after the first weekend in August, which may seem early. Then when the plant signals that it needs more water (it'll dry out faster), that's usually the first sign that it's beginning to wake up and start its growth cycle. Greater demands for water mean more cellular activity has started. At this time, I begin giving weak applications of water-soluble plant food each time I water my plants.

Plant tags and houseplant directories sometimes tell you when the plant requires its dormant period. If they don't, just watch the plant for signals.

Fertilizer Don'ts

Here are a few things to keep in mind when using houseplant fertilizer.

- **Don't fertilize plants just after they've been repotted.** Plants can't take up nutrients for a few weeks just after being repotted—they're trying to adjust to what's just been done to them. But there's another reason why you don't need to fertilize after repotting: Fresh potting soil will have some food in it—enough for two to three months. Read the ingredients on the bag to see what's in your potting mix.
- **Don't fertilize sick plants.** A sick plant isn't interested in eating when it's sick (just like you). Your efforts will be wasted, and you could do more damage than good—the plant may die. Let it get back to its normal condition before you resume feeding—and then feed it only with one-quarter the recommended strength.

- **Don't fertilize just after you buy a plant.** Your plant has already been fed. There's enough food in the potting soil for at least two months, and probably longer. And if you look closely, you'll probably see some time-release food on top of the soil. Feeding a plant just after you've bought it is like landing in Austria after having lunch on the airplane and immediately heading for the nearest restaurant. Give your plant time to acclimate itself to its new surroundings.
- **Don't fertilize plants that are resting.** From September to February most houseplants take a rest, as I've discussed. During this time, plants won't put on much (if any) new growth. They also don't eat. Why should they? They aren't growing or expending any energy—they don't need food (they're smarter than we are). Same for the outdoor plants, trees, and shrubs—they go dormant, too. When plants prepare for their dormancy cycle, they don't want or need food.
- **Don't fertilize your plants with the full-strength recommendation.** Use one-quarter the recommended strength listed by the fertilizer manufacturer. Otherwise, the plants won't use it all, and you'll be adding to the fertilizer salt buildup.

TIPS

Wax your pots

Susan, a gardener friend, always plants her African violets in clay pots—she says they look better and more natural. But as time passes and the leaves touch the rim of the pot, they die. Some of them look like something's been cutting into the side of the stems. Fertilizer salts are the problem.

Here's a trick: Melt some clear wax on top of the stove in a pan that you can throw away. Using a throw-away paintbrush, paint the rim of each pot with a thick coating of wax. This will protect the leaves. Clear wax isn't noticeable and won't detract from the look of the plant.

Save willow water

Do you grow pussy willows in your yard and bring stems indoors for a spring show? If so, here's a trick you might want to try. You can use this tip on rooted houseplant cuttings, houseplant seedlings, or seedlings for your vegetable garden.

Put the pussy willow cuttings (or cuttings from any member of the willow family) into a vase of water. After you've enjoyed their beauty for about three weeks, take them out of the vase and use the willow water to water your seedlings. Like packaged commercial rooting compound, willow water contains indolabutyric acid (IBA) and promotes strong growth.

Removing fertilizer salts from pots

Beginners are always the proud recipients of old, scarred clay pots, which have been given to them by seasoned gardeners in order to encourage the novices' interest. Have any of you beginners noticed white patches on your "new" pots? These are fertilizer salts. They seep through the walls of clay pots and appear as white patches on the sides, but they also form thick, crusty deposits around the rim. You can get rid of the salt buildup and sterilize your pots at the same time. Try this solution:

1. Scrub each pot with a steel wool pad or stiff brush. Dip the pad into a solution of 1 part vinegar to 1 part water as you scrub.
2. Rinse the pots.
3. Soak the pots in a solution of 1 part bleach to 9 parts water for 30 minutes.
4. Rinse the pots again and reuse.

Don't fertilize herbs

Herbs that you grow indoors don't need fertilizing if you intend to use them for cooking. The more you fertilize herbs, the less fragrance and essential oils you'll get. These plants are used to roughing it. Many of them originally came from hot climates where there was little rainfall in the summer. They aren't used to being coddled—their genetics doesn't run that way. Coddle them and you won't get the true essence of the herb—you'll miss the potent fragrance and the memorable flavor.

S ooner or later you'll have to do it. Pot or repot. There's an old word I don't hear anymore: shifting. For years, we used to say that we were "shifting up" or "shifting down" when we repotted. This meant that we were shifting our plants from one container into another, using a larger or smaller size pot. I still hear the term potting-on, but not as much. Now we just call it repotting. With the passage of time, a little charm has been lost here, I think.

It would be better for your plants if you always repotted in the spring when you set everything outdoors (if you are one of those who welcomes summer camp for your houseplants). I'm making this suggestion for three reasons.

First, houseplants have begun their spring growth cycle by then and will take to repotting better than if they were repotted in the fall. I've taken liberties with plants in the spring that I wouldn't dream of attempting in the fall—and the plants have permitted it. This is because they're so intent on getting a running start out of the gate and putting on a quick spurt of growth that they don't seem to notice you're pestering them. You can't mess up a repotting job in the spring as you can in the fall. A difficult division such as a clivia *(Clivia miniata)* would certainly best be done in the spring.

Second, if you repot a plant that's in dormancy, the roots aren't actively

growing, so they won't fill their new pot quickly, and they won't use the water in the soil. Thus, the soil stays damp for longer periods of time, and eventually, root rot sets in.

Finally, repotting in the spring means the plants will have filled their new pots with full growth by the time you take them indoors to show them off in the fall. If you wait to repot until the fall, the plants won't fill out their new living quarters when you take them in—they'll look puny in the larger pot. The plants look overpotted—meaning the containers are too large, so the plants look lost in

Plants prefer to have snug quarters. The plant on the left is swimming in its pot, but the plant on the right fits well.

the expanse of space. You'll have all winter to sit and look at your mistakes, because the plants aren't going to grow then—they're dormant. This won't show off your skill as a houseplant gardener.

Here are some things to ask yourself to determine if your plant needs repotting:

- Are roots growing out the drainage hole of the pot?
- Does the plant wilt a day or so after flowering?
- Is the plant putting on new leaves that are smaller than usual?
- Are the lower leaves yellowing?
- Does the plant look as if it's splitting or breaking the pot?
- Does the soil dry out so quickly that frequent watering is necessary?
- When you knock the plant out of the pot to examine its roots, do the roots look so massed that very little soil is visible (maybe it even looks as if there isn't any soil left in the pot)?

- Have you just purchased a plant that looks far too big for its pot?

If the answer is yes to any of these questions, your plant is potbound and needs repotting. If you don't know the answer, then knock the plant out of its pot and look at the roots. My rule of thumb is this: If 50 percent or more of the pot is taken up with roots, it is time to repot.

I used to have two monster plants: a crown-of-thorns (*Euphorbia milii* var. *splendens;* when it bloomed each year, it was absolutely covered with little red flowers), which was 5 ft. tall and 3 ft. wide, and a mother-in-law's tongue, also called snake plant (*Sansevieria trifasciata* 'Laurentii'; it always produced the most fragrant white flowers), which was more than 28 years old, 5 ft. tall and 2 ft. wide. I never repotted them until they broke the clay pots they were in. Then I knew each was ready to move up an inch in pot size.

Garden centers and nurseries usually carry plants that are so well grown that they require repotting soon after you take them home. You usually do get what you pay for, and then some. Confirm your suspicions by knocking the plant out of its pot. One look at the roots will tell you if you need to repot. Beginners won't be stumped by this; it'll look obvious.

If your plant produces flowers, there's no immediate need to rush and repot. And *don't* repot the plant if it is in the process of flowering—wait until it finishes. This is because flowering plants love to have their roots be in tight places, and the plants may not bloom unless they are. Geraniums and clivias are good examples of such plants.

Signs that it's time to repot

A plant will tell you that it needs repotting by sending roots out drainage holes, wilting easily, breaking the pot, and producing small or yellow leaves.

Pot Size

In general, repot a plant into a pot that is one size (1 in.) larger than the one it was in. For spreading plants and hanging baskets, use a pot that equals one-third to one-half of the *diameter* of the plant. Plants do much better if they're underpotted rather than overpotted. A big pot with a small plant in it will guarantee that the soil will stay wet all the time. Now remember what we said about roots needing air: If they don't get air between waterings, they begin rotting; and this, in turn, shows up above ground in the condition of the leaves.

Water-logged roots do not occur only in houseplants. I see this when I'm working with outdoor plants in landscaped areas. Gardeners who plant yews (*Taxus* species) in their yards invariably place them near a downspout. When our southern spring rains come, the plants sit in water for hours because of our heavy clay soil. This causes large, fully developed yews to give up the ghost in a matter of days. In fact, they actually begin their decline after sitting in water for only a few hours. When you make mistakes like this, your pocketbook and landscape are hurt as well as your plant.

There is no hard-and-fast rule about when to repot, yet there are *indications* of when a plant needs a bigger pot, and we've talked about these.

Overpotting and its consequences

Overpotting simply means that the plant has been potted into a container that's too big for it. If properly cared for, plants produce only a certain amount of growth each year and no more. This is why it's always a good idea to shift up only one pot size when it comes time to repot. If you shift up two pot sizes, the plant won't

When the roots start circling the bottom of the pot, it's time to give them more soil in larger quarters.

produce the root growth to fill the pot. And you know what happens next: The soil stays damp longer, the roots begin to rot, and the plant dies.

Many beginners make the mistake of putting a plant into a pot that's too big for it, thinking that they won't be bothered with repotting for a few years. Wrong. The beginner won't *have* a plant to be bothered with before long. The following is a likely result: If you turn the overpotted plant out of its pot, you'll be greeted with few roots and a smelly mass of goo.

In case this should ever happen to you, wash all of the soil from the roots. Then cut off the dead or damaged roots, and repot into a *smaller* pot using a good-quality light potting soil. There's a chance that you may be able to save the plant.

You need to do a little
light surgery for the benefit of the plant before it
goes into a larger pot.
Use a sharp knife and
make four cuts on each
side of the root ball from
the top to the bottom.
Pierce several of the
large roots. There are
reasons for doing this:

- The roots will stop growing in a circle

- The plant will be stimulated to grow new roots
  to fill in the freed-up
  space

Then repot the plant, following the instructions on
pp. 70-71.

The cast-iron plant
grows so slowly that it
may not need repotting
for years. (Photo by
Janet Loughrey.)

Plants that like to be potbound

Yes, there are plants that like to be potbound (see the following list). These
homebodies don't want to be bothered
unless absolutely necessary. Letting them
break the pot they're planted in is a good
way for them to tell you when they want
to have a little more room.

- Amaryllis (*Hippeastrum* species)
- Angel-wing begonia (*Begonia coccinea*)
- Bamboo palm (*Chamaedorea erumpens*)
- Bird-of-paradise (*Strelitzia reginae*)
- Bird's-nest fern (*Asplenium nidus*)
- Boston fern (*Nephrolepis exaltata* 'Bostoniensis')
- Brake fern (*Pteris* species)
- Cast-iron plant (*Aspidistra elatior*)
- Chinese evergreen (*Aglaonema modestum*)
- Clivia (*Clivia miniata*)
- Lily of the Nile (*Agapanthus africanus*)
- Moses-in-the-cradle (*Rhoeo spathacea*)
- Ornamental pepper (*Capsicum annuum*)
- Paper flower (*Bougainvillea glabra*)
- Rubber plant (*Ficus elastica*)
- Sago palm (*Cycas revoluta*)
- Screw pine (*Pandanus*)
- Song of India (*Dracaena reflexa*)
- Ti plant (*Cordyline terminalis*)
- Tree ivy (× *Fatshedera lizei*)

Shapes and sizes of pots

If you like the classic rimmed clay pot,
you'll find it in various sizes. And you'll
also find it in different shapes. But don't
be put off by this. The pots are shaped
differently for a reason, and there are
only a few shapes that you have to
become acquainted with.

For instance, there's the azalea, or fern,
pot. Azaleas and ferns look better when
planted in these pots, and the stocky
shape is perfect for their shallow roots.
But these pots also are called "half-pots,"
and because spring-flowering bulbs (such
as tulips and daffodils) can be grown in
these pots, some gardeners call them
"bulb pots" (confusing, isn't it?). Azalea
pots are broad or stocky, and they're only
three-quarters as deep as the regular-size
pot. The standard clay pot is noticeably
deeper and rather slender looking. To
further confuse you, there are also
shallow clay pots called "bulb pans,"
which also are used for growing bulbs
(such as tulips and daffodils).

Determining the *size* of a pot is simple.
The pot is measured by the diameter
inside the rim. For example, a 5-in. pot
has an inside rim diameter of 5 in. The
height of the pot is about the size of its
rim diameter.

For clay pots, the sizes range from
1½ in. to 15 in., with pots increasing ½ in.
in size as they step up from 1½ in. to 9 in.

The step-up size is larger than ½ in. for pots over 9 in., and there is no 11-in. pot. You need a lot of luck to find pots between 12 in. and 15 in.

Don't become overwhelmed by all of these sizes. The more you use clay pots, the more you'll be able to tell an azalea pot from a bulb pan. Most of us don't use all of these sizes anyway—we repot into a narrow range of sizes, hovering in the 4½-in. to 9-in. range.

So far I've been talking only about clay pot sizes. That's because clay pots come in more standard sizes than plastic pots. (Plastic pots come in all sizes and shapes imaginable.)

You can remember this, however: Regardless of which pot size you choose, make sure the pot:

- Has a central drainage hole or several small holes at the bottom
- Is the right size for the plant that will go into it
- Is a color that won't detract from the plant or its surroundings
- Comes with a drip saucer, if it's to be set on furniture

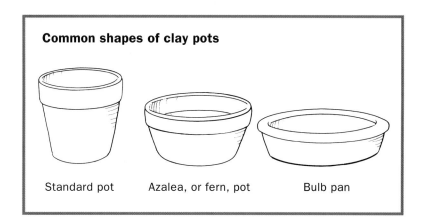

Common shapes of clay pots

Standard pot   Azalea, or fern, pot   Bulb pan

As much as I love clay pots, they have one problem. Their clay saucers don't provide any protection for your good furniture. Clay is porous; this means that the moisture from the pot seeps through to the saucer, which seeps through to your furniture. The clay saucer is bound to leave an ugly, indelible ring on a prized piece, so be warned. There are, however, clear, light plastic saucers (usually found at garden centers or even in the floral section of grocery stores) that you could use in place of the clay ones. Some are so clear that you barely notice them, and they are a little taller than the clay saucers so that they hold even more water.

Types of Pots

Besides coming in different shapes and sizes, pots are available in a wide variety of materials and for specific purposes. For many, however, the biggest dilemma is deciding between clay and plastic.

Clay or plastic?

Most houseplant gardeners of the "old school" prefer the classic clay pot. I include myself in this group. These pots have been used for centuries, and one reason they're still so popular (aside from the fact that plastic is a new invention) is that they are porous; they absorb water but also allow both water and air to pass

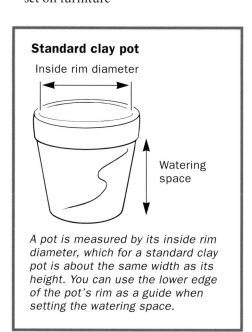

Standard clay pot

Inside rim diameter

Watering space

A pot is measured by its inside rim diameter, which for a standard clay pot is about the same width as its height. You can use the lower edge of the pot's rim as a guide when setting the watering space.

CHARACTERISTICS OF CLAY AND PLASTIC POTS

Characteristic	Clay Pots	Plastic Pots
Porosity	Porous, water and air flow through the walls	Not porous, hold moisture
Fertilizer salt buildup	Easily noticeable on sides of pot and rim	Less noticeable; none on sides, a little on rim
Watering	Must be watered more often	Don't have to be watered as often
Root rot	Doesn't easily occur; overwatering doesn't happen often—you have to work at it	Easily occurs from overwatering
Weight	Heavy; won't fall over	Lightweight; will tip over easily
Aesthetics	Classic looking, typical of the garden; natural terra-cotta color blends in well with nature	Cheap and unnatural looking; don't blend in well with nature
Drainage	Have drainage holes; some large pots may not, but holes can be drilled with a masonry bit	Have drainage holes; some large pots may not, but holes can be drilled
Hanging	Hang with orchid hangers or wire (drill holes with a masonry bit)	Usually come with hangers; metal hangers can be purchased; good hanging baskets because they're light
Size and shape	Various sizes	Wide variety of shapes, surfaces, and colors
Drip saucers	Must be bought separately	Often come with the pot and may be attached to it; can be bought separately; available in several sizes
Use with furniture	Hold moisture	Don't release moisture; can be set on furniture.
Breakage	Break, chip, and crack easily, but the pieces can be used for crocking	Less likely to break, but will become brittle if left in the sun for long periods of time

through the sides. This means there is little chance you'll overwater your plants, because water is always evaporating through the clay walls.

If you want to prove that air and water pass through the sides of a clay pot continually, try this experiment: Fill a sink with water and set a dry clay pot into it. You'll immediately notice bubbles escaping around the pot. This means that it's drinking—taking on water. At the end of an hour, remove the pot from the sink. It'll feel heavy; its color will be darker, and if you rap on it, you'll hear a dull sound as opposed to the high *ping* you would hear when the pot was dry.

Because clay absorbs water, beginner gardeners now are warned not to repot into a dry clay pot. When you water your plant after repotting, the dry pot takes its share of water from the surrounding soil and leaves the plant roots with what's left—and that's very little. This also means that clay pots must be watered more often than plastic pots. Clay is just like a sponge—when it becomes dry, it gets thirsty.

But your choices aren't limited to clay or plastic. Pots are also made of other materials you might like better: plastic foam or polystyrene, outdoor paper, wood, fiberglass, and glazed earthenware are some examples. You even can make your own little seed-starting pots out of rolled newspaper. There are also pop-up pots (peat moss "dollars" that expand in water), cell packs made of plastic foam, cell packs made of hard plastic, and . . . well, you get the idea. You won't run out of choices.

You even may decide to stand firm with the old standbys—clay pots. So, for the uninitiated, the chart at left gives the dirt on clay and plastic pots—the two most common types.

Pots for hanging plants

Personally, I like to see the old wire hanging basket. They were lined with long-fiber sphagnum moss and filled with light potting soil. They were meant to be used only outdoors or in areas where they could drain freely onto the surface below. These really were baskets for holding plants. They were prettier and more natural looking than the cheap, artificial-looking plastic ones you see today. The baskets had to be watered constantly during the summer and were allowed to drip-dry, so the best places for them were outdoors under an arbor or tree, in the greenhouse, on the patio, or in a garden room that had a stone or brick floor.

The plastic ones came along so that plants could be taken indoors and cared for without causing water damage. You don't have to water anything in plastic as often as in clay because plastic holds moisture for a long time. But I thought then and still think today that something got lost in the transition from the natural look to the plastic look. I don't like trading good taste for convenience.

To me, plastic is just plain ugly. It's an artifact of the new techno-throwaway society that values convenience over beauty—the kind of society that values the perfect, impersonal, sterile, rubber-stamped product over the imperfect, moss-covered, aged character of a product fashioned by the human hand and weathered by nature and time. It seems that little thought is given to the more natural, more classic way of displaying floral beauty—with all its

blemishes. One gives up much for convenience.

But take heart. You do have a third choice of "basket" that will hang. I discovered this when I kept everything in clay pots and wouldn't convert to plastic. You *can* hang a clay pot. There are two ways to do it.

Use orchid hangers Have you ever been to a conservatory and seen orchids hanging in slatted baskets filled with moss or bark? Keep looking around, and you're bound to see orchids in clay pots hanging around, too. But the hangers look different from the hanger of a plastic hanging basket.

Orchid hangers can turn any rimmed clay pot into a hanging basket.

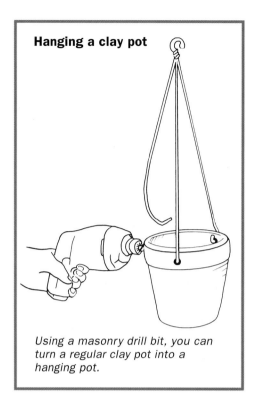

Hanging a clay pot

Using a masonry drill bit, you can turn a regular clay pot into a hanging pot.

Orchid hangers are meant to attach to clay pots *with rims.* You slide the rim of the pot between the spike and clamp of the orchid hanger. The long metal clamp on the outside of the rim grabs the rim of the pot and holds it. The other side of the hanger (the spike) goes down into the pot. The opposite end of this long hanger forms a hook from which the pot hangs.

I used to see orchid hangers everywhere 35 years ago, but you may have to get them from mail-order catalogs now. I recommend you find a catalog specifically for hobby greenhouse enthusiasts. These hangers are still out there, because people still grow orchids. Mine are made of thick metal and will last for many decades to come.

Drill your own holes Here's a method for hanging clay pots that don't have rims. Use a masonry bit to drill your own

holes. I've found gorgeous clay pots I simply had to have, but they didn't have rims.

My husband (always handy with tools and quick to ride to the rescue) drilled the three holes needed and attached the same thin metal hangers that you see on plastic hanging baskets. You can find these hangers at garden centers, and they're not expensive.

Now, having said all this, two things remain, and they may prove to be the deciding factor for you.

- **Clay pots dry out fast.** This means that you'll have to water more. You may not want to hang clay pots if you're away from home a lot.
- **Clay is heavy.** The wire will hold your pot—no fear there. But will the surface that you suspend it from hold the pot? Remember, a wet clay pot is even heavier than a dry one.

The best way to handle these two drawbacks is to hang your clay pots from the thick, heavy structure of an outdoor arbor that creates a shaded area, so that plants don't dry out so fast. Hanging pots indoors presents no difficulties as long as they are hung securely.

Self-watering pots

For many people, watering time is enjoyable. It's a time when they can slow down their day; touch, smell, and look at their plants; check for insects trying to set up house; and even find a surprise flower bud or two.

But some houseplant gardeners are on the go constantly and just don't have the quiet time to spend communing with their plants. If you're one of these people, a self-watering pot was made for you. People with African violet collections also use these pots because they deliver a constant source of moisture and

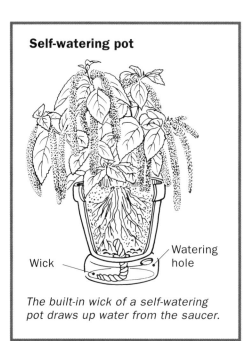

Self-watering pot

Wick   Watering hole

The built-in wick of a self-watering pot draws up water from the saucer.

nutrients to plants that are expected to stay in bloom but that dry out quickly.

Self-watering pots have their own water supply, a little reservoir that furnishes the root ball with constant moisture and food at a rate that the plant can use. The pots keep the soil evenly moist, and because tiny amounts of food are always available, there's no feast-or-famine syndrome, which I talked about in Chapter 6.

The principle behind these pots is simple. The pots work by capillary attraction—wicking. They use a fibrous wick to draw the water from the reservoir up into the soil. Here's an example of how wicking works: Half-fill the sink with water. Hang the tip of a hand towel over the side of the sink so that it touches the water. Leave and come back in one hour. You'll find that the water has moistened most of the towel. The water has been wicked up into the towel. This is the same principle behind self-watering pots.

Self-watering pots come in a variety of shapes and sizes, but they are more expensive than regular pots. However, don't let the price put you off this watering method because you can make your own self-watering pots. (I'll tell you how in Chapter 12.)

How to Repot

New gardeners generally don't like to think about repotting. They put it off until their plants are so root-bound that there's little soil left in the pot, or masses of roots begin trying to escape out of the drainage hole. These gardeners are afraid they might damage or kill their plants. But plants are pretty resilient, and you have to work at it to mess up a repotting job. Repotting is also quick, so don't despair if you have a lot of it to do.

Just remember a few things:

• Choose a pot that's only one size larger than the pot your plant is in.

Adding drainage holes to a pot

Wood

A decorative ceramic container can be converted into a pot with the use of a masonry drill bit. A piece of wood helps to prevent cracking.

How to repot a plant

1. Use pot shards, large pebbles, or sphagnum moss to cover the bottom of the pot, then place a little soil over it.

2. Place the plant inside the new pot and add potting mix.

3. Firm the soil around the plant. Leave ½ in. of space from the soil surface to the pot rim.

How do I get a large plant out of its pot so I can repot it?

Lay the pot on its side and rap the sides with the palm of your hand, a rubber mallet, or a block of wood. You may need another person to pull the plant out of its pot as you rap on the pot.

• Make sure the pot is clean. If it isn't, clean it using the method on p. 73.
• Make sure your pot has a drainage hole in the bottom. If it doesn't and your pot is clay or glazed, use a masonry drill and make some holes.
• If you're using a new clay pot, soak it several hours before you pot into it.

Now here's the procedure.

1. Crock the pot. This means cover the drainage hole with pieces of broken clay pot (called "crocks"), pieces of brick, or some large pebbles or stones. This is done to keep the soil from escaping through the drainage hole, at the same time allowing excess water to flow out freely. Don't use screening or paper towels—the soil will escape eventually.

2. Add a little potting soil to cover the bottom of the pot. Those of the old school will prefer adding the following materials after crocking: 1 in. of pebbles, a little charcoal (not grilling charcoal), and a thin layer of crushed leaves or peat moss. Don't feel obligated to add these. Adding a good, porous potting soil or mix is all you need do in this step.

Now, set this new pot aside. It's time to deal with the plant.

3. Thoroughly water the soil and the plant. Let the water drain out.

4. Invert the pot and remove the plant by knocking the rim of the pot on a surface. If the plant is stubborn about coming out, rap a little harder and repeatedly. If it still refuses to cooperate, use a sharp knife and encircle the perimeter of the pot along the sides.

Then invert the pot and rap it again. The plant should come out.

Remove the old crocks (if there are any) from the root ball of the plant. With the plant now out of the pot and inverted, set the old crocks aside for future use. Keep the root ball intact.

5. Set the plant into the center of the new pot. Fill in around the plant with good, porous potting soil. Press firmly around the outer edges of the pot, adding more soil until it comes up to the base of the plant—*to the height it came up to when the plant was in its old pot.*

Try to judge the spacing here. You should stop adding soil when you are ½ in. from the rim of the pot; this will give you room to water without overflowing the pot.

I like to add ½ in. of coarse builder's sand to the soil before I get to the empty space below the rim (see p. 37). Some longtime gardener friends of mine use a thin layer of mulch instead of the sand, but you can leave this out if you like.

6. Water the plant carefully. Use warm water to settle the soil. Put the plant in a shady area for a week until it recovers, and gradually move it back to its old sunlit position.

Potting style has changed over the years. People in the nursery business don't even crock their pots anymore. When they pot or repot, they simply pour in the good potting soil, set the plant, and firm the edges. They put a little time-release fertilizer on top of the soil, and that's it.

The reason for this simplified potting routine is probably because the potting soils and soilless mixes we get now are so much better than what we had years ago. They're much lighter and do not retard drainage. You had to amend the old stuff if you didn't want dead plants—it was such a heavy mix. At that time, new

houseplant enthusiasts just beginning the hobby didn't know that the potting soil wasn't good—they'd never had anything to compare it to. And they didn't know how they could amend it and make it better. They had to read up on the subject, which is how I learned.

Those early days of houseplant gardening were trying, because if you lived in an apartment, you had to find a place for bags of peat moss, charcoal, potting soil, fertilizer, sand, and other amendments for potting. There was also the difficulty of finding a place to pot. When I lived in an apartment, I always used the little grassy area outside the front door. Those little apartment kitchens didn't (and still don't) allow for much movement or storage, and there's always the terrible cleanup to follow.

If you live in an apartment, let me save you a headache. The potting instructions here told you to bring the soil up to ½ in. below the rim of the pot. *Follow this exactly.* I learned from experience that if you overfill a pot, the excess will always be a pain to clean up. When I lived in an apartment, *everything* went to the sink or tub for watering, showering, and grooming. And, of the two, the tub was faster, easier to clean up, allowed plants a place to drain, and gave them a brief humidity boost.

How to Topdress Large Plants

Now what do you do with those monster plants that have lived with you for decades? They've outgrown their pots countless times and have begun to put on weight in their old age. Are your *Monstera, Brugmansia, Spathiphyllum, Dracaena,* and *Dieffenbachia* plants becoming too huge and too heavy to move out the front door for repotting?

Good news: You don't need to move them in order to repot them. You can

---

I've tried everything, and I can't get my large palm out of its clay pot. Help!

In this case, you may have to break the clay pot. The pot will be easier to break if it is dry. Use a hammer and lightly tap the side of the pot until it begins to crack. Then, pull the pot shards away and remove the plant. Keep the broken pot to use as crocking for future potting jobs.

How do I get a stubborn plant out of its plastic nursery pot?

If you've tried the methods mentioned here and they don't work, you'll have to cut the pot away from the root ball. This isn't as difficult as it sounds. Nursery pots are made of thin plastic and are very easy to cut— nursery workers have to do this all the time. Use tin snips or sharp shears for this task.

How to topdress a plant

1. Use a spoon to remove the top inch or so of soil, being careful as you uncover roots near the surface.

2. Add new soil to replace the old, then water the plant.

topdress them. *Topdressing* simply means removing a few inches of topsoil from the pot and replacing it with fresh good-quality potting soil.

I have several old fellows, and every year they get topdressed. This method isn't as good as a complete repotting—but it's the next best thing, and there aren't any alternatives. A large plant can stay in confined quarters for years without being repotted. The only thing you need to do is give it a little fresh potting soil each year.

I have a huge 20-year-old ponytail plant (*Beaucarnea recurvata;* the mother of all *Beaucarnea* plants) and a monster of a night-blooming cereus (*Epiphyllum oxypetalum*). They need this treatment each spring. The plants can't be moved, and topdressing must be done in place.

This is how to do it.

1. Gently remove 1 in. or 2 in. of soil from the surface. An old spoon comes in handy here.

2. Work around any roots on the top of the soil, being careful not to damage the roots. Have a container handy so you can dump the soil into it (you'll throw it away when you finish). Whatever you do, don't use a paper bag; it will *always* tip over or close up just as you're about to dump a spoonful of soil into it.

3. Add good potting soil and water in the soil. You won't need to feed your plant right away because there'll be enough nutrients in your potting mix to lightly feed it. Besides, you don't want it to continue to grow through the roof. The idea is to have a large accent plant (and a valuable accessory) for many years, not to have it for just a few years and then be forced to toss it because it has grown too large.

Preventing sour, smelly soil

In the repotting instructions, I mentioned that some gardeners add charcoal to their pots. Charcoal is good for potted plants. Years ago, pea-sized charcoal (not the charcoal used for outdoor grilling) was used in pots to keep the soil from smelling sour. It was thought that the charcoal sweetened the soil and absorbed odors and fertilizer salts. In those days, I used charcoal in potting and repotting on a regular basis, and I think the idea behind its use is a good one.

Gardening charcoal (meant for use in pots) used to be packaged in small plastic bags, and in some locations you can still find it. I sometimes see it at local department stores in the houseplant area near the goldfish tanks. You also might find it at your garden center or order it from a gardening catalog.

Sterilizing pots

If you reuse clay and plastic flowerpots, you'll need to sterilize them before each use. This suggestion isn't just something to keep you busy while your asparagus grows: Sterilizing is meant to kill the fungus responsible for doing in otherwise healthy houseplants. The formula given on p. 60 for removing fertilizer salts from the rims and sides of clay and plastic pots also works for sterilizing.

Sand mulch

Have you ever watered a plant and had the peat moss and perlite float around in the pot and cling to leaves? I stopped this from happening by adding sand to the pot when repotting.

Use coarse builder's sand (not beach sand) and add it up to the last ½ in. below the rim of the pot. This not only will keep the soil from floating around, but also will weight down a pot that's too light and keep it from tipping over. Use this trick when you pot up amaryllises for Christmas bloom.

I've been told to root-prune my large indoor tree to keep it from becoming root-bound. Should I do it?

I'd think long and hard about this. If you were to slice down through the roots on the outside of the root ball all the way around, envision what you would have left. Then look at the top leaf growth that would have to be supported by the remaining roots. I think you can guess what would happen. The roots would be unable to supply the top growth with everything it needs, and the plant would begin to die.

Here's a simple solution: Prune the top growth as well. The general rule is if you take away roots, you also should take away proportionate top growth.

CHAPTER EIGHT

INSECT PESTS AND DISEASES

A garden room filled with healthy houseplants can be an exquisite addition to your home. (Photo by Mick Hales.)

Modern indoor gardening is multidimensional, and what makes it so are the numbers of atriums, greenhouses, and other indoor spaces devoted to growing plants. Homeowners can create their own green worlds indoors because they now have what they didn't have before: an ideal growing environment. This is due to a larger expanse of strong or bright light that is easily controlled; air-conditioning, which can be shared with the rest of the house; heating, which also can be shared with the rest of the house; ceiling fans; stone floors; and easily concealed outlets everywhere for humidifiers.

The indoor-gardening revolution has also created business opportunities. Mail-order companies gladly will send you a catalog offering everything a houseplant gardener could possibly want, including insect pest information and products. Because indoor gardeners don't just grow pothos (and its insect pests) anymore, pest control is a more complicated problem. When the limited growing conditions afforded by a small living-room window was the only option available, plant varieties and their pests also were limited. Now people are growing vegetables and rain forest plants once thought hard to grow. Along with these new plant options has come a wider range of insect pests not found in homes before. Who worried about indoor whiteflies in the 1950s and 1960s?

Fortunately, a good thing has come out of the explosion of interest in gardening: environmentally safe pest-control products. These effective products don't harm people, the environment, or pets.

Controlling Pests and Diseases

Insect pests and fungus problems are likely to bother the new generation of plants and plant room gardeners, but I've had success with a few insect pest remedies, and I'll share these with you later in this chapter. One of these remedies is meant to be used in the greenhouse only: the use of beneficial insects, which become permanent residents and little helpers in the fight against insect pests. The other remedies can be used in both the greenhouse and indoor plant room. In fact, your great-great-grandmother may have used some of them with excellent results long before many of the toxic chemicals, dusts, sprays, and pellets now on store shelves were invented.

Do the remedies in this chapter work? I've used all of them, and they've worked for me. But one thing is certain: *Persistence is the key.* A one-time spraying won't do the job.

Even the off-the-shelf products must be reapplied, because overhead watering washes them off; insect pests multiply fast, and just when you think you've beaten them, they reappear. So a *routine* application of a remedy will be needed to stay on top of things.

If you're a beginner to growing houseplants, you may think that because your plants are indoors you needn't worry about insect pests or fungus problems. *This couldn't be less true.*

Because your plants are indoors, you may be so unconcerned about pest problems that you don't notice you have them until it's too late and your whole plant collection is infested. Indoor conditions are ideal habitats for insect pests to grow, multiply, and thrive. You don't see many spider mites outdoors in the dead of winter. But let the furnace kick in and indoor air dry out, and you've got the perfect environment for an infestation to begin.

Keeping close company with your plants and putting your hands on them as often as possible will help you head off problems. Whenever you water your plants, clean up decayed foliage around them, prune any areas that don't appear healthy, and look at the leaves and stems.

Look closely on the tops and undersides of leaves. Most pests are tiny, but their damage is great—they can cost you a treasured plant collection if they're allowed to get out of hand.

Notice any yellowing or mottled leaves; webbing between the leaf and stem (the axil); and dark, unhealthy areas on leaves or stems. Turn the leaves over and look for egg masses, clusters of insects, and insect droppings, which usually show up as tiny black specks.

Sometimes simply washing the plant with a mild soap either in the shower or at the sink on a regular basis will clean up your pest problem. Other times, further measures must be taken.

If you use safe remedies persistently, I think you'll find that they're just as efficacious as the more expensive (and

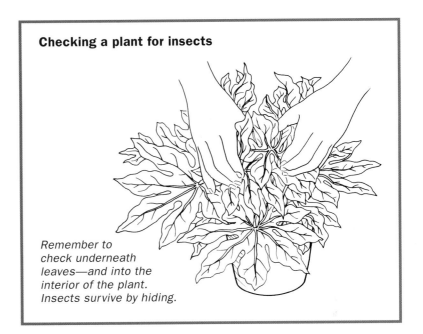

Checking a plant for insects

Remember to check underneath leaves—and into the interior of the plant. Insects survive by hiding.

more toxic) products you find on the market. Most of the ingredients called for can be found around the house.

Know when to say good-bye

If you ever have a plant that is so heavily overcome by insects or disease that you aren't able to return it to good health, *get rid of it*. Sooner or later you'll have to do it anyway—plants (like our beloved pets) don't live forever.

Up to this time, you've invested money, energy, and time in a plant collection you've been proud of. It's been a learning experience and a journey well worth its occasional setbacks. Friends and family have enjoyed looking at the beauties of nature with which you've surrounded yourself, and them.

But now it's time for caution. It's better to be cautious than lose your entire collection to insect or disease problems. If infestation occurs in a few plants, immediately separate them from the rest of your collection and treat them apart. Handle them only *after* you tend to your

Aphids come in several colors and are usually found on new growth. If left unchecked, they multiply rapidly. (Photo by Alan L. Detrick.)

other plants so that you won't unknowingly transfer pests and disease to your healthy collection.

But if your efforts don't return those plants to their previous optimal good health, say good-bye to them. And don't bury them in your compost heap—you could still spread the problem. Put them in the trash.

Insect Pests

Here are the most common insect pests found on houseplants.

Aphids

Description Aphids come in different colors: black, gray, brown, light yellow, and green. Sometimes called plant lice, these soft-bodied pests multiply faster than rabbits. They suck plant juices and excrete a sticky substance (called "honeydew") on the leaves and stems of plants.

The honeydew allows sooty mold to grow (see p. 81), and it also attracts ants. In fact, if you have ants indoors, they'll be drawn to the honeydew deposits, and then you'll have ant colonies in your flowerpots. Outdoors, aphids are a problem, and the ants don't help. They actually herd the aphids, moving them about, so that they'll produce honeydew for the ant colony.

Symptoms
• Plants appear tired.
• Stems and leaves, especially on new growth, may be distorted.
• Leaves curl, discolor, and display reduced growth.
• Flowers are damaged.

Signs they're there Aphids can be present any time of the year on houseplants. You may feel the sticky honeydew on leaves and stems. Look for them clustering on buds, leaves, and stems.

Susceptible plants Any plant with soft stems and leaves is susceptible to aphid infestation. The following plants are particularly vulnerable:
• Cyclamen (*Cyclamen persicum* hybrids)
• Impatiens (*Impatiens* species)
• Nasturtiums (*Nasturtium* species)
• Persian violets (*Exacum affine*)
• Roses (*Rosa* species)

Solutions Try wetting down your plants repeatedly to get rid of aphids. If it's winter, give your plants a shower indoors every two weeks. If it's summer, hose them off outside.

You also can try removing the aphids with your fingers.

Other solutions to try:
• Commercial insecticidal soaps
• The Old Soap Bath Remedy (see p. 84)
• All-Purpose Insect Spray (see p. 84)
• Ladybugs and lacewings (see pp. 86-87)

Fungus gnats

Description Fungus gnats are a nuisance more than anything. They are tiny, slow-flying insects that hover just over the surface of the potting soil. Adults lay their eggs in the soil, and the hatched larvae feed on decaying plant roots. Experts disagree about whether the gnats will damage live roots on mature plants. If the gnats are present in large numbers, they will damage live roots of seedlings.

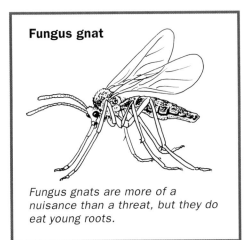

Fungus gnat

Fungus gnats are more of a nuisance than a threat, but they do eat young roots.

cotton fluff because of the cottony, waxy sac of eggs that the female attaches to the end of her body. Their outer coating repels water (and insecticides). Like aphids, mealybugs excrete a honeydew and suck plant juices.

Symptoms
- Leaves are spotted or deformed.
- Leaves are yellow.
- Infested plants look unsightly, with noticeable white patches all over stems and crotches.

Signs they're there Mealybugs excrete honeydew, which you can feel when you touch the plant. You easily can see the bugs—they look like white cotton. Look for them clustering together on plant stems, in crotches where leaves attach to stems (the axils), and under the leaves. They're also visible on the roots.

Susceptible plants Almost any plant is susceptible to mealybug infestation, but the following plants are particularly vulnerable:
- African violets (*Saintpaulia* species)
- Azaleas (*Rhododendron* species)
- Cacti
- Citrus trees (*Citrus* species)
- Gardenias (*Gardenia* species)
- Geraniums (*Pelargonium* species*)
- Succulents

Solutions For root mealybugs, try a soil drench (see p. 85).

For the mealybugs on the leaves and stems, try an alcohol swab: Dab the leaves and stems with an alcohol-drenched cotton ball. Some people mist their plants with a solution of alcohol and water. The alcohol cuts through the mealybug's repellent outer coating.

Wipe off any egg sacs hiding under the rim or on the bottom of the pot.

Mealybugs look like bits of cotton stuck in the crevices of leaves and stems. (Photo by Derek Fell.)

Symptom
- Seedlings grown in soil with added organic matter wilt.

Signs they're there You'll see the adult fungus gnats flying just above the surface of the soil.

Susceptible plants Fungus gnats like organic matter such as peat moss and peat-based potting soils. The following plants are particularly susceptible to infestation:
- African violets (*Saintpaulia*)
- Ferns

Solutions One method of getting rid of fungus gnats is to try to keep the soil a little drier than you have been.

Other solutions to try:
- Commercial soil drenches
- Two Soil Drenches for Fungus Gnats (see p. 85)
- Homemade Sticky Traps (see p. 85) used at the base of the plants

Mealybugs
Description Mealybugs are sluggish and soft-bodied pests closely related to scale insects. They're oval in shape, about ¼ in. long, and white. They often appear as

Other solutions to try:
- The Old Soap Bath Remedy (see p. 84)
- All-Purpose Insect Spray (see p. 84)

Red spider mites

Description These pests are sometimes referred to simply as spider mites. They are actually spiders with eight legs instead of six, which characterizes true insects. Spider mites are tiny, and it's difficult to see them. But you'll see their damage: They suck the sap from plants. They love a hot, dry environment, which is typical of many homes, especially in winter.

If you have spider mites, get rid of them as soon as you can, because they'll take over your entire plant collection if they go unchallenged. You'll be battling spider mites throughout the year if you don't set up a schedule of monthly soap baths or spraying.

Symptoms
- The top of the leaf surface becomes mottled, which changes to pale yellow; soon the leaf begins to curl and, finally, falls off.
- Any new growth appears stunted.
- Flowers may appear discolored or blackened.

Signs they're there Red spider mites can be present any time of the year in the greenhouse or plant room. You can see their tiny webbing between the stems and leaves (the axil) of your plants. Webs also appear on the undersides of leaves.

Susceptible plants Just about everything can be attacked by spider mites, but the following plants are particularly plagued by them:
- Cucumbers, strawberries, and dahlias (for those with greenhouses)
- English ivy (*Hedera helix* hybrids)

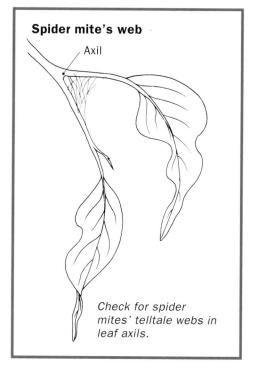

Spider mite's web

Axil

Check for spider mites' telltale webs in leaf axils.

- Fuchsias (*Fuchsia* species)
- Roses (*Rosa* species)
- Spider plant (*Chlorophytum comosum*)
- Violets (*Viola* species)

Solutions Spider mites don't like humidity or moisture. So keep an electric humidifier in your plant room or small greenhouse—within several feet of your plant collection—and keep the reservoir filled to the proper level constantly. The advantage of this solution is that plant foliage won't stay wet. There's no way your plants can come down with a fungus infection unless you water them too much; and, if you keep them in clay pots, that probably won't happen anyway.

Some houseplant growers have a mist system that comes on to raise the humidity in the greenhouse at certain times of the day. This is fine, but misting in the house doesn't work well. Everything, including the dog, ends up getting misted. In winter, the mist is

This webbing is the work of spider mites, which are almost invisible to the naked eye. (Photo by Derek Fell.)

evaporated by the furnace when the heat comes on. And do you really want your houseplant foliage staying damp all winter? You have enough to worry about without fungus attacks. If it's winter, give your plants a shower indoors every two weeks. If it's summer, hose them off outside.

Other solutions to try:
• Commercial insecticidal soaps
• The Old Soap Bath Remedy (see p. 84)
• All-Purpose Insect Spray (see p. 84)

Scale insects

Description Most scale insects are oval in shape and brown in color. They look like flat or raised bumps on the stems and leaves of your plants. You can see the young insects move, but the mature ones are stationary. The difficulty with these insects is that their waxy coating doesn't allow sprays to penetrate well. Scale insects excrete honeydew, and they suck plant juices.

Symptom
• Leaves turn yellow and may fall off.

Signs they're there Scale can be present any time of the year in the greenhouse. Look for them on the undersides of leaves. They excrete honeydew, which you can feel when you touch the plant.

Susceptible plants All plants are susceptible to scale; the following plants are particularly susceptible:
• Citrus (*Citrus* species)
• Ferns, especially bird's-nest fern (*Asplenium nidus*)

Solutions One method you can use to get rid of scale is to pick the adults off your plants by hand.

Scale insects, though seemingly motionless, extract liquids from plants and leave a telltale trail of honeydew.

Other solutions to try:
• Commercial insecticidal soaps (for young scale)
• The Old Soap Bath Remedy (see p. 84)
• All-Purpose Insect Spray (see p. 84)

Whiteflies

Description These fast-moving insects look like tiny white moths. Whiteflies are usually found clustered on the undersides of leaves, where they also deposit their eggs. The larvae are almost translucent. Whiteflies are difficult to get rid of. They excrete honeydew, and they suck plant juices. If you summer plants outdoors, whitefly egg clusters can come in with plants that are getting ready for their fall rest.

Symptom
• Leaves are mottled and yellow.

Signs they're there Whiteflies can be present any time of the year in the greenhouse. Look for them on the undersides of leaves, where they're easy to see. When they're disturbed, they fly up around the plant. Whiteflies excrete honeydew, which you can feel when you touch the plant.

Susceptible plants The following plants are particularly vulnerable to whitefly infestation:

- Ageratums (*Ageratum* species)
- Azaleas (*Rhododendron* species)
- Basil (*Ocimum* species)
- Chrysanthemums (*Chrysanthemum* species)
- Fuchsias (*Fuchsia* species)
- Geraniums (*Pelargonium* species)
- Gerbera daisies
- Lantanas (*Lantana* species)
- Poinsettias (*Euphorbia* species)
- Tomatoes

Solutions Whitefly larvae can be controlled with an alcohol swab: Use a damp cloth soaked in alcohol to wipe off the undersides of the leaves.

Try shaking the plant and then vacuuming up the flies as they hover above the plant.

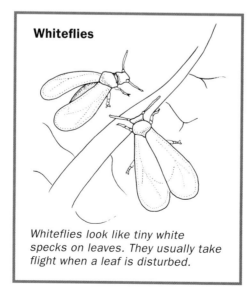

Whiteflies

Whiteflies look like tiny white specks on leaves. They usually take flight when a leaf is disturbed.

Another solution to try:
- Homemade Sticky Traps (see p. 85)

Plant Diseases

Here are the most common diseases found on houseplants.

Powdery mildew

Description and symptoms Powdery mildew is a fungus that leaves white or gray powdery patches on leaves, flowers, and stems. The leaves and flowers may be covered with it. It first appears on the tops of older leaves—older leaves being more susceptible than younger ones. The leaves covered with the mildew turn yellow or brown, twist, and eventually fall off. Complete defoliation may result; however, plants seldom die from this fungus. Nearby plants can be affected.

Causes
- High humidity and low temperatures
- Poor air circulation
- Overwatering

Susceptible plants Some begonias and any plant exposed to high humidity and low temperatures.

Solutions Here are some simple ways to control powdery mildew: Pick off all the affected leaves, give the plant more light, and improve the air circulation. Try to keep temperatures as even as possible.

After touching plants with this disease and before touching any other plants, wash your hands thoroughly. Or handle diseased plants last, after your other plants have been tended.

Other solutions to try:
- Commercial insecticidal soaps
- The Old Soap Bath Remedy (see p. 84)
- Spray for Powdery Mildew (Fungus) (see p. 85)

Sooty mold

Description and symptoms Sooty mold is a fungus. It is attracted to and grows on the sticky honeydew excreted by sucking insect pests such as mealybugs, aphids, scale insects, and whiteflies. It looks like black soot and feels sticky. The black coating reduces the growth of the plant by blocking needed sunlight. The leaves of an affected plant turn yellow and die from this lack of light. The presence of sooty mold should alert you to the fact that some insect pest is on your plant.

Causes
- It grows on the honeydew excreted by insect pests.

Susceptible plants Citruses and any plant exposed to high humidity and low temperatures.

Solutions It is important to get rid of the insect pests excreting the honeydew. Wash the leaves regularly with warm, soapy water. Remove any yellow leaves.
   Another solution to try:
- The Old Soap Bath Remedy (see p. 84)

Stem and crown rot

Description and symptoms Stem and crown rot is caused by a soilborne fungus *(Pythium)* that attacks the roots. The stem or crown of the plant becomes soft, slimy, and rotten; and affected plants don't grow. Crown rot causes dull black or brown leaves, which decay from the center of the plant to the outer edges. The lower leaves may yellow and fall off. The roots die and rot, and the entire plant may wilt and die. Stem and crown rot spreads rapidly throughout the plant.

Rosemary is especially susceptible to powdery mildew. Good air circulation helps prevent the formation of spores, which spread the disease. (Photo by Alan L. Detrick.)

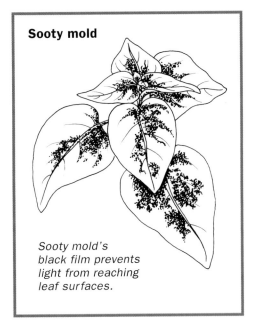

Sooty mold

Sooty mold's black film prevents light from reaching leaf surfaces.

Causes
- Low temperatures
- Soggy potting soil
- Overwatering
- Poor drainage
- Poor air circulation

Susceptible plants
- African violets (*Saintpaulia* species)
- Cacti
- Echeverias (*Echeveria* species) and other rosette-shaped plants
- Impatiens (*Impatiens* species) and other plants with soft stems
- Persian violets (*Exacum affine*)

Solutions To take care of stem and crown rot, first take a look at your potting soil—it must not be allowed to remain wet. Make sure it drains well, and try drying out the soil more than you have been between waterings.

If the soil is too heavy, repot your plant with a lighter soil; and be sure to choose a smaller pot. Increase the air circulation around your plant.

Never pot a plant into a dirty pot because stem and crown rot could result. Sterilize your pots with bleach (follow the formula for removing fertilizer salts on p. 60). After touching plants with this disease and before touching any other plants, wash your hands thoroughly. Or handle diseased plants last, after the others have been tended. If all else fails, the only solution may be to throw a diseased plant away.

What to Do if You Suspect a Problem
The first sign of insect invasion is usually sticky leaves. Several pests leave a trail of sticky honeydew behind. This should warn you that they have arrived. If the

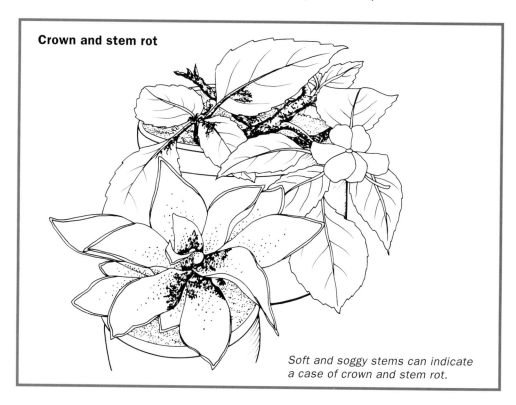

Crown and stem rot

Soft and soggy stems can indicate a case of crown and stem rot.

problem is disease related, look at your cultural practices—are you giving the plant what its culture requires?

Here are some steps to take if you suspect a pest or disease:

1. Isolate the affected houseplant. Get it away from your other plants so that the problem doesn't spread. Locate the source of the problem and determine how widespread it is.

2. Select a remedy (from this chapter or elsewhere). Don't use it immediately; instead, test a small portion of the plant first to see if any "burning" results. The test area may look brown, as if it were burned. If burning is going to occur, you'll see it within two days. Some plants resent insecticidal soaps, and may resent the soap-based remedies given here. Ferns, palms, and jade plants are a few that voice their dislike of soap.

3. Use the chosen remedy if the plant exhibits no signs of burning.

4. Keep the plant isolated for one month to see if the problem returns.

5. Put the plant back in its usual place if there are no signs of infestation or disease. Repeat Steps 3 and 4 if the problem returns. Remember: *Persistence is necessary.* Keep the plant isolated until it's clean, then put it back in its place.

Remedies for Insect Pests and Diseases

The liquid dish-washing soap used in the recipes that follow should be *mild.* No heavy-duty grease fighters should be used, and don't use a detergent. Soap cleans surfaces and dries up bacteria. But it's also a surfactant and allows a solution to stick to the plant it's sprayed on so that it doesn't wash off as quickly. This is a trick used by nursery workers and

agricultural extension agents—people who deal with sprays on a regular basis. The remedies I'll give you are safe and won't harm your children, pets, or home environment. These remedies don't leave foul odors or damage furniture. But if you're ever skeptical about a remedy being sprayed indoors, take the plants outdoors, one at a time, and spray them there. You can set them in the shade to dry and then bring them in.

Save your milk jugs. I've found that a thoroughly washed out plastic milk jug works well for making up a gallon of solution.

Applying a Remedy

There are two ways you can apply a solution to your plants: spraying it onto them or dipping them into it.

Spraying plants Many remedies call for the ingredients to be sprayed on the affected plants. Some of the solutions can be applied via a pump-up sprayer. A pump-up is great for greenhouse use because it'll cover a large area. If you plan to use this large sprayer, increase the ingredients in the recipes given (just as you would a cooking recipe). Mix the ingredients, pour the solution into the pump-up, and spray your plants.

If you don't have a greenhouse, make up the recipes as given and put the solution into a mister spray bottle.

Some remedies tell you to "spray to the point of runoff." This means that you should spray until the liquid runs off the leaves and stems.

Dipping plants Sometimes you'll need to dip your plants into a solution to get rid of pests and diseases. Dipping works well for small potted plants. Mix the ingredients in a large pail. Make enough of the solution to cover all of the leaves and stems once the plant is immersed.

Here's how to dip a plant:

1. Hold the root ball in the pot with your fingers.

2. Tip the plant over and dip it into the pail of solution.

3. Soak the foliage and stems either by plunging the plant in and out of the liquid or by swishing it around in it.

4. Carefully remove the plant from the pail and set it upright to dry.

Reapplying solutions Plants in a greenhouse or in your home aren't being constantly rained upon, so these sprays should last longer if you don't wet the foliage. But if you shower your plants or water them from above with a watering can, you will need to reapply the remedy, just as you would if you were using the remedy for plants kept outdoors.

Dipping a plant

Dipping a plant's foliage into a soapy insecticidal solution ensures that all foliage is evenly covered.

The Old Soap Bath Remedy

This is the simplest and oldest method of insect pest control for houseplants. Remember when Grandmother threw her soapy dishwater out the back door and onto the rose bushes near the house? She knew what she was doing. Soap solutions wash away insects, insect eggs, dust, and dirt.

Application: Greenhouse or garden room

Using: Hand mister, pump-up sprayer, dipping

Repeat treatment: Once a week, if needed

Warning: Don't use this remedy on hairy plants such as African violets or begonias.

Ingredients

1 gallon warm water
1 tablespoon mild liquid dish-washing soap

Procedure

1. Start with the water.
2. Add the soap and mix thoroughly.
3. Spray or dip the affected plant.
4. Leave the solution on the plant for 2 hours.
5. Rinse the plant with warm water.

All-Purpose Insect Spray

This remedy contains alcohol and soap. You'll actually increase the effectiveness of your soap solution by mixing it with rubbing (isopropyl) alcohol. The alcohol will penetrate the insect's waxy coating and allow the soap to kill it.

Application: Greenhouse or garden room

Using: Hand mister or pump sprayer

Repeat treatment: Twice a month, if needed

Warning: Don't use alcohol by itself as a spray; it will burn the foliage.

Ingredients

1 quart warm water

4 tablespoons rubbing alcohol

1 teaspoon mild liquid dish-washing
soap

Procedure

1. Start with the water.
2. Add the soap and alcohol, and mix
   thoroughly.
3. Spray the affected plant to the point
   of runoff.
4. Leave the solution on the plant for
   2 hours.
5. Rinse the plant with warm water.

Spray for Powdery Mildew (Fungus)

The practice of using baking soda in a
solution to decrease fungus conditions
has been known to the medical
community for some time. This idea also
works in treating powdery mildew on
mini-roses, lilacs, and other flowering
plants. But, once again, prevention is
best. Use it *before* you begin to have
problems.

Application: Greenhouse or garden
room

Using: Hand mister, pump-up sprayer

Repeat treatment: Twice a month, if
needed

Ingredients

1 gallon warm water

5 tablespoons antiseptic liquid hand
soap

3 tablespoons baking soda

Procedure

1. Start with the water.
2. Add the soap and baking soda, and
   mix thoroughly.
3. Spray over and under the leaves of
   the affected plants to the point of
   runoff.
4. Let the plant dry (do not rinse).

Two Soil Drenches for Fungus Gnats

The larvae of the fungus gnat feed on the
plant roots and crowns of African violets.
This remedy is often given by African
violet enthusiasts as a sure cure for their
ailing plants.

Application: Greenhouse or garden
room

Using: Soil drenching

Repeat treatment: Once a month, until
you no longer have the problem

Ingredients for drench #1

1 quart warm water

2 tablespoons commercial insecticidal
soap

Ingredients for drench #2

1 quart warm water

1 teaspoon liquid household bleach

Procedure for both drenches

1. Mix all the ingredients together.
2. Drench soil of your affected plants.
   Do not wet the foliage.
3. Because the plant was watered with
   the remedy, don't water again until it
   needs it.

Homemade Sticky Traps

Do sticky traps work on whiteflies and
other insects? Greenhouse enthusiasts tell
me they work only too well—they catch
beneficial insects and pests. If you intend
to use sticky traps in your plant room,
don't let looks bother you. You can easily
tuck them in and around the pots or
hang them out of the line of vision.
Whiteflies are attracted to the color
yellow and will be drawn to your traps.

Application: Greenhouse or garden
room

Warning: *Don't use these traps if you
release ladybugs, lacewings, or other
beneficial insects in your greenhouse.*
These inexpensive traps will catch
aphids and whiteflies in both the
greenhouse and plant room.

Homemade sticky trap

Whiteflies and aphids are drawn to yellow sticky cards.

For use in the greenhouse: Make several traps. Drill a small hole at the top and use fishing line to hang them throughout the greenhouse. Check the traps weekly to see if they are full of insects and require cleaning and refreshing with oil.

For use in the garden room: Make a trap for each affected plant. Attach 6-in. lengths of coat-hanger wire to the back of each board, using strong tape. Place the boards in the pots of the affected plants by inserting the wire into the potting soil. Place the traps out of the line of vision where they won't be seen by visitors.

Materials
Spray paint, school bus yellow
¼-in plywood cut into 4-in. by 6-in. rectangles
Mineral oil

Procedure
1. Spray-paint the front and back of the plywood pieces and let them dry.
2. Coat the front and back of the plywood with mineral oil.
3. Place the boards in your greenhouse or plant room.

When the boards are full of insects, wipe them clean and refresh them with mineral oil.

Ladybugs and Lacewings
Beneficial insects should be used in the greenhouse only. But don't release these beneficials if you intend to use sprays. The sprays will kill them as well as the pests they eat.

Ladybugs
Ladybugs can be used to control aphids. Many gardeners who own a greenhouse like to turn ladybugs loose and let them keep the plants clean. I don't recommend that you do this in the house; use the ladybugs in a controlled environment such as a greenhouse, which is not connected to your family's living space.

In your greenhouse, ladybugs will continue to prosper and reproduce, as long as there's a food source. They dine

Ladybug

Ladybugs are the heroes of gardens and greenhouse since they eat many plant pests.

on aphids (which they like best), scale, spider mites, mealybugs, and whiteflies.

When you buy ladybugs, make sure you have a ready food source of insect pests waiting for them. It's also important that you provide them with water when they arrive at their new home, because they're usually trucked in and are thirsty after their long trip. Garden centers mist them off with a gentle spray of water when they arrive, and you should, too, when you get them home.

If you buy from a mail-order company, order them before fall weather arrives; and when they arrive through the mail, do the following:

- Gently and lightly spray the ladybugs with a mister bottle of water.
- Keep them out of the sun.
- Wet down the area (soil and foliage) where they will be let loose.
- At nightfall, open the bag and lay it at the base of one of the infested plants.
- Let them crawl out at their leisure, no need to shake them out.

By morning, your ladybugs, for the most part, will be out of the bag and feeding on the affected plants. They arrive hungry and ready to do their work.

If you wait until winter is over to buy your ladybugs, many garden centers near you will have them in late spring.

Lacewings
Lacewings are equally effective in the greenhouse, and should be ordered before winter sets in. While ladybugs can tolerate some cold weather, lacewings can't, and it's possible to lose your shipment once the temperatures drop.

If your lacewings or ladybugs are very lethargic when you receive them, they may have been damaged due to cold temperatures in transit.

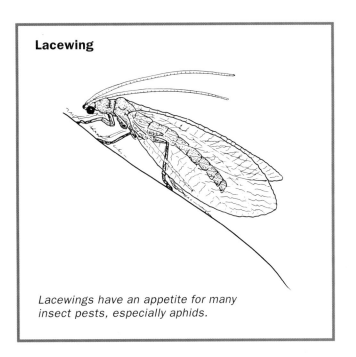

Lacewing

Lacewings have an appetite for many insect pests, especially aphids.

TIPS

I've set up the remedies in this chapter like recipes. Like most good cooks who write their observations in the margins of their cookbooks, you should get in the habit of making notations in the margins of this book—jot down your comments, observations, and how you've tailored the recipe to your needs. Experienced gardeners will tell you that a good part of gardening (indoors and out) is observation and acting upon those observations. You'll save yourself a lot of grief if you jot down what worked for you in your particular situation. You'll come back to those notes time and again for the same remedy in the future.

CHAPTER NINE

PLANT SOURCES AND SELECTION GUIDE

I look for houseplants everywhere, but I buy from only a few places. These are places I've grown to trust for their insect-free, well-cared-for plants. It's taken me a few years, some bad experiences, and a little money to compile my list, but I now know whom I can trust to deliver a good product. You'll have to follow the same course of action if you're to build a good collection.

It isn't difficult finding suppliers that stock disease-free, well-grown plants. In order to save you time, I've listed some places you might start with.

Plant Societies and Clubs

Whenever your local hobby greenhouse club, houseplant club, perennial society, or herb society has a plant sale, *go to it!* These people know what grows well because they grow it. And since many members have greenhouses or plant rooms and grow hundreds of plants, they're familiar with plant culture and can shed light on any question you have. They also have tons of printed information to give you (usually free) for the asking, can recommend the best plant books to read, and can tell you about their garden room or greenhouse if you're interested in constructing or buying one.

Club members are a tireless lot. They love talking about plants, and will give you specifics about their favorites. These are people with firsthand experience. They've encountered all the setbacks, dealt with disease and insect problems, and can tell you (in detail) what steps to follow, what works, and what doesn't. You can't fool them—they know their stuff, and they know misrepresentation in the gardening business when they see it. Most of them aren't beginners.

These enthusiastic gardeners will stand for hours talking to you about plant culture if you have the time—it's their job to inform and create interest in plants. They'll probably give you a phone number or two, which will put you in touch with others nearby who can give you information.

The plants they sell usually are plants they've grown themselves. They may have raised them from seed or taken offsets from plants that have become too large and needed dividing. And their plants are usually small. This is a plus for you, because it's better to start with a fairly small specimen that can easily acclimate itself to your environment. Large plants don't settle into a new home as well—they're used to the setting they just came from. I've had large plants that have taken a full year to settle down, and during that time, very little new growth was put on.

Accompanying each plant will be a plant tag identifying it by its botanical and (usually) common name. Societies and clubs are fanatics about labeling plants. They know the difficulty of locating a plant if the common name is all that's given.

Botanical names will make it easier for you to locate precise information on the plant you bought. Common names change, depending on what part of the country you're in, and confusion always results. But botanical names don't change (not often, anyway)—they're universal. In other words, you can buy a plant labeled *Kalanchoe fedtschenkoi* 'Marginata' in Belgium just as reliably as you can buy a plant labeled *Kalanchoe fedtschenkoi* 'Marginata' in Kansas. This same plant goes by the names of Palm Beach bells, South American air plant, lavender scallops, and perhaps others.

If a botanical name is ever changed, it'll be written up somewhere. I remember in the 1970s when pothos was changed from *Scindapsus aureus* (a pronounceable name) to *Epipremnum aureum* (an unpronounceable name). Most plant directories mentioned the name change, but there were a few that hadn't made the jump to hyperspace and kept referring to pothos by its old name. Well, most of the public did too, but not the plant societies. They knew better.

Plant societies and clubs also bend over backward to sell pest-free plants—plant hygiene is a serious matter to these people. They know only too well how an indoor infestation of whiteflies can get out of hand quickly and damage prized specimens. If you have time, members will treat you to a few horror stories of their own in dealing with insect pests. Battling indoor pests goes hand in hand with growing houseplants. But they'll tell you that much of the battle is using preventive measures. Club members can give you tips on preventive care for your own collection. They've all learned little tricks over the years that aren't necessarily in books or magazines

Plant societies and clubs will be glad to give you information on how you can become a member of their organizations, and you can gain a lot by joining. Annual dues are minimal, and clubs usually meet once a month. Often, there are lectures given by members or special guests (I've spoken to many of these groups) that will add to your knowledge of growing plants. Members plan field trips and view private plant collections—some of them are collections of fellow club members. There are also opportunities for you to exchange plants or seeds—this is a great way to increase your own collection.

One day you might find yourself on the other side of the sale table as a member of the club talking to an enthusiastic beginner about houseplants.

Garden Shows

Invigorating garden shows usually take place in late winter or early spring (February to April)—just the time of the year when you're ready for daffodils and chirping birds.

Growers from in and out of state sell their plants there. It's a good way to get a

Plant societies offer small but high-quality and unusual plants at their sales.

jump on spring, because the garden centers won't have received their shipments yet. You'll come away with loads of herbs and other plants that can't be set out until the weather warms up. But you can set your little gems in the bright indirect light of a south- or west-facing window until it's time to repot them into larger pots and set them out (if you are one who likes to summer plants outdoors).

Garden shows last four or five days. If the show begins on a Thursday, attend it then or on Friday, if possible—it'll be less crowded than on the weekend. And plan to arrive just after opening. This way you can take all the pictures you want without having people pass in front of you. To help guide you through the show, you'll receive a map of the entire layout after you purchase your ticket at the door. You'll also get a list of all the gardens and where they're located, a list of all the nurseries and companies represented at the show, and a list of all the stalls, restrooms, and dining areas.

As you enter, you'll be struck by two things: the smell of mulch mingled with fragrant blooms and the huge indoor expanse, all parts completely landscaped as if they were outdoor gardens. In fact, one building won't hold everything— these shows are usually staged in one or more large buildings that may or may not be connected.

The theme of the show is expressed in the design and choice of plants you'll see, and each year the theme changes. This means that the local nurseries, garden clubs, Master Gardener Associations, and garden centers that participate must come up with garden design and plant groupings that best reflect the year's

theme. Some of the plants used in each design are the new beauties being offered for the year and usually can be purchased from the exhibiting nursery or landscape company. There's always a representative of each exhibiting company on hand to answer questions about the exhibit or the plants used in the company's design.

Everything truly looks like a storybook wonderland. The entire floor space is covered with sample gardens, one after another. The color and fragrance of flowers, trees, shrubs, blooming bulbs, and cascading vines are a welcome sight after the long gray winter.

But there aren't just sample gardens to view. You'll also be able to attend hourly lectures (often for free) on various gardening subjects, from how to make scented herbal soaps to growing plants for a butterfly garden. Sometimes, visiting garden writers are in town and are asked to lecture and sign copies of their book.

After you've been through all the sample gardens, jotted down design ideas for the spring, taken all your photos, heard a lecture or two, grabbed so-and-so's new garden book (signed, of course), and had something to eat, it's on to the booths. On sale at the booths you will find everything from birdhouses, to garden clothing, to hot tubs. You may even encounter a cooking demonstration. Local plant societies also will be selling their plants, and local botanical gardens usually exhibit their books and offer information about tours.

Each little booth you come to will have representative plants that each nursery or garden center sells. I prefer to visit the family-owned nursery stalls because I can find plants there that I won't find that time of the year at garden centers. The growers may be local or they may be from out of state. Their stock is usually a mixture of large and small plants, expensive and inexpensive. There's always variety.

Be sure to come back a few hours before closing time on the last day of the show. Many companies that design the huge garden exhibits sell their plants then, as they begin to break down exhibits and clean up the area. You can often get houseplants, trees, shrubs, bedding plants, bulbs, perennials, and herbs at greatly reduced prices. The reason for selling is simple: Why cart something back when you can sell it? Bring your truck!

Plan to spend the entire day when you visit a garden show. Set out early and take a thick carrying sack with handles to set your purchased plants into. Take your camera, pencil, and paper; wear sensible shoes; and be prepared to be enchanted.

Florists' Shops

Florists' shops are excellent sources for houseplants. After all, they're in the business to sell them almost exclusively. Some of the most robust, full-growth specimens are found here. Prices may be high, but you get what you pay for.

The quality of florist houseplants can't be denied. They always will be first-rate plants because so many of them are presented as gifts. And because florists deal almost exclusively with flowers and houseplants, their plant material must be in excellent condition—their existence depends upon it.

Depending on the size of the shop, I've found that the selection is usually small but good. You'll see beautiful houseplants grown under optimum conditions and properly labeled with instructions explaining their care. They'll be insect-free and grown to perfection. And they probably will have fertilizer granules already in the pot so that the plant won't demand any immediate care outside of watering. This is sensible because so many houseplants are given to hospital patients.

I have a favorite family-owned florist shop that's been owned by the same family since the 1950s. But this shop is different from most because the owners also have a landscaping business and sell herbs, perennials, annuals, seed, bulbs, and vegetables, as well. Whenever I go there, I have to discipline myself—I set a time limit; if I didn't, I'd be there for hours looking at all the handmade wreaths, centerpieces, dried arrangements, and jars filled with sweet-smelling potpourri.

Yes, the price will be a bit high no matter what you buy—it always is when you're dealing with a shop whose merchandise is so exclusive. But if you have the money, houseplants (or anything else) bought from a source like this are well worth it. And there's always the chance that you may be given a florist-shop plant for some special occasion. Then you can judge the quality for yourself.

This, by the way, is how some enthusiasts actually get started in their houseplant hobby. They receive a plant while in the hospital, and it cheers them up. They bring the plant home and discover that it continues to cheer them months later. They put the plant on a table in the sunroom during the dead of winter, and they're hooked. Outside the window, there's a perennial bed buried under a temporary white blanket of snow, but on the table sits the promise of many green tomorrows.

Chain Stores

Chain stores carry a wide range of plants—both indoor and outdoor varieties. The houseplants are usually located indoors and in an area all to themselves. Recently, chains have built huge greenhouses to show off their new stock of orchids (which seem to be in vogue now) and other houseplants. Bromeliads are increasing in supply and beginning a resurgence after a few decades of disinterest. This is a good indication that houseplant interest is rising and will continue for some time.

Many of the houseplants in chain stores come from growers located in Florida. Most of these nurseries are now back on their feet after the hurricane disaster of several years ago that wiped out much of the houseplant industry in that area. Floridians are resilient gardeners and have bounced back with new offerings and more choices that will tantalize.

Chain stores are likely to have all the old standbys and some of the new plants just coming out. But you'll have to develop a strategy when shopping at a chain store. Try to get to the store when the shipment of new plants is taken off the trucks. That way, your plant will be fresh from the grower and won't be sitting on the shelf week after week, sharing pests and fungal diseases with its neighbors. Houseplants crowded together in an area are like children in school. You know how it is. One child gets sick, and they all get sick.

Pricewise, houseplants are a bargain at large chain stores. But I stress the advisability of buying them as soon as they arrive. They seem to go downhill in a few weeks, and there goes your bargain.

Now it's time for a word of warning: *Never buy a sick houseplant* with the idea that you can take it home and resuscitate it. It won't work.

In some stores you'll see discount areas filled with plants that look ratty. This is the "sick, neglected, and ready to croak" area. Yes, the price will be right. It'll be marked down low enough to entice you—that's the idea. But you risk a lot when you feel sorry for a sick plant or get suckered into buying it because it seems like such a steal. It's not worth it.

Listen. If you set any of those plants among your other healthy houseplants, you risk infecting *them* as well. And, anyway, you want a collection that you won't mind showing off—not one you'll end up having to apologize for. One sick plant can spoil the overall picture you're trying to create.

If you're a beginner, don't start your lifetime hobby with poor specimens. Your interest will soon wane when all your good intentions and effort don't pay off after months of TLC. If you're a seasoned houseplant gardener, you know better—you've already learned your lesson. You'll save your money for those pricey plants you simply *must* have.

Remember, you're a discriminating plant connoisseur with an eye for beauty and form, not a nursemaid.

Mail-Order Companies

There are numerous catalogs you can get that are filled with houseplants to order. Catalogs are a great way to locate those plants that are hard to find. Many of the plants are tropicals, so make sure you read about the sun and temperature requirements, and have the proper environmental conditions in your home to grow them.

The catalogs and mail-order companies will be listed (along with address and phone numbers) in the back of most of the better gardening magazines. The companies will be glad to send you their latest catalog and, if you are a new customer, they may even give you a discount certificate for use toward your first order.

For the most part, these companies are eager to please. The good ones will do everything they can to assist you because they want continued business. If your plant dies or arrives in poor condition (which is not usual), they'll offer you a replacement plant if you bring the problem to their attention. If they can't replace the same plant, they should offer you a refund.

And don't throw up your hands and go looking for small boxes and packing peanuts; you don't have to send back the plant you're having trouble with. These reputable companies will take your word for it without fingerprinting you. But you do need to have your invoice ready when you call them. They'll want your invoice number and/or customer account number. The plants you order are under warranty, so to speak, for a specified time (this varies with companies). Fortunately, most companies have a toll-free number to handle these inconveniences. It'll be noted somewhere on your invoice.

Now, what about price? The prices are good. But be aware that the plant you purchase will be small. There are good reasons why companies prefer to send small plants:

• The companies can keep their prices down and their business up.
• Small plants are easy to package and transport.
• Small plants hold up better than large plants as they travel; less moisture is lost in transpiration.
• Small plants withstand the shock of arriving without much soil around their roots, and they handle transplantation and recovery quicker and better than large plants.

• Small plants are always recommended as start-off plants because as they grow, they can slowly acclimate to your environment. Larger plants don't acclimate well at all. It takes them months, even years, to settle down.

Mail-order companies want you to be a successful houseplant gardener. They know that if you become discontented or lose interest, their business drops. So many of them prepare helpful fact sheets on plant culture. You may find one of these culture sheets or cards tucked in the package with your plants. Read it and save it until you become fully acquainted with your plant's culture. This shouldn't be new to you, because I mentioned the same thing earlier in this book when I recommended that you study the plant tags that come with store-bought plants.

For the most part, your ordered plants will arrive in good condition. But how

Inspect mail-order merchandise carefully as soon as it arrives on your doorstep.

you care for them from that point on is crucial. Here are some suggestions:

1. Open the packing box. Do this as soon as you receive it and examine your plants without delay.

2. Assess the condition of your plants. If you see that your plants are in poor condition, call the company. Give them the invoice and customer account number, explain what has happened, and ask for a replacement. If this isn't possible, ask for a refund.

3. Pot your plants. If your plants made the journey in good condition, they can be potted. Select small pots and follow the company's instructions for potting. Don't overpot or you'll quickly lose your plants to rot.

4. Water the plants. Water thoroughly with warm water, but don't feed them. Give the plants a chance to make the transition and settle down.

5. Keep your plants out of any direct sun or strong light. Within a few days, gradually introduce them to the light level they require.

6. Begin feeding. After several weeks, start them on a mild feeding schedule. Use soluble houseplant food at one-quarter the manufacturer's recommended strength.

7. Don't overwater. Be careful at this stage not to overwater because root development may not be large enough to handle continually damp soil.

8. Watch the plant closely. If you see any signs of yellowing, decrease watering—let the plants dry out a little more between waterings.

Mail-order nurseries usually include a plant tag with your plant, identifying it by its botanical name. Don't lose this, because you need to know exactly what you have. You can't depend upon common names if you intend to order more of the same plant or if you want to collect plants from the same family.

The good thing about houseplant mail-order companies is that during the year, they usually have plant sales. They cut their prices on so many offerings that they may send you another (smaller) catalog so that you can take advantage of the slashed prices. You'll probably find some great buys.

Family-Owned Stores

Family-owned stores may not always be large, but they're excellent places to find houseplants. In fact, if you grow annuals, perennials, or other outdoor plants, you can do all of your shopping in this one place. Family-owned garden stores have a good assortment of just about everything.

These businesses aren't usually in the propagation business—their stock is from local and distant suppliers. You're assured of getting good stock, because plants that don't arrive in good condition

A family-owned garden store is usually stocked with high-quality merchandise, and the staff can offer plenty of plant culture hints.

are sent right back where they came from and orders are canceled. A family-owned business cannot afford to sell a poor product if it wants to stay in business. The company must please its customers.

Try to time your visits to the store so you are there when the trucks arrive. The freshest plants are those that are being unloaded. The owners won't mind telling you when to be on the lookout for the next truck. They want you there.

There are all kinds of neat things at these stores. You'll find stuff strictly for the gardener: hand tools, labels of all kinds, plant hangers, lifelike silk plants, fertilizers, garden clothing, small indoor fountains, dried arrangements and swags, seed, bulbs, wildflower mixes, herbal topiaries of all kinds for your plant room, and . . . well, you get the idea.

The prices aren't as good as they are at the chain stores, but you're likely to find plenty of unusual plants or hard-to-find plants. So *au diable d'avarice!* (to hell with money), as the French say. Search for something that no one else grows. I always find something I haven't seen before or spot a plant I've been trying to locate for ages. Don't depend upon chain stores for this—they deal in the usual.

For a few years now, family-owned stores have been including one-hour lectures (sometimes in a series), workshops, and demonstrations as part of their effort to bring in the customer. It's worked well. It's also produced a much more savvy gardener. Free material and a good lecture once every few weeks will pack the store. I've often spoken at these places and come away having thoroughly enjoyed the afternoon. Some stores have even set aside a special lecture area to accommodate crowds of over 200.

And there are children's workshops, too. In fact, family-owned stores often cater to the entire family. There is usually a child-care area, which leaves parents free to shop while their children play or attend their own little garden workshops.

I think the larger chain stores are beginning to catch on now—slowly. Recently, I've noticed a few of them offering lectures to gardeners and houseplant enthusiasts as a way of stimulating business.

Visit a family-owned garden store, and you'll see the owner and members of the family actively at work with the public, educating, advising, and guiding purchase decisions. The entire family is usually knowledgeable about the newest plant material for the season and its cultural requirements. Rarely will you find people with this information at chain stores. Workers there usually only water or sell the plants—they haven't the vaguest idea how to care for them.

There is also a different atmosphere about a family-owned business, something in the air that you don't notice in chain stores. People enjoy being there. Members of the family and the people they hire are friendly and eager to help. They enjoy talking to the public and view interruptions as a necessary and important part of their work. Most of them know about all the plants they tend in their area and would be glad to advise you. If there's a special plant that you've been looking for, you can ask the store to order it. They believe that if you're interested in it, others will be too.

Over the years, I've made it a point to do business in family-owned stores, and the part that always impresses me is how the owners are always ready to go the extra mile for their customers, some of whom they've known for 20 or 30 years and regard as friends. This may very well

The leggy, spindly growth on the plant on the left is a sign of poor light conditions and care. Choose a plant with compact, stocky growth, such as the plant on the right.

Purchase plants with healthy green leaves that are spaced close together.

be the key to their success at a time when so many chains view their customers as faceless entities in possession of money.

Selection Guide

If you shop in a good store, the quality of your houseplants usually will be good. Here are some things to keep in mind as you choose your plants. After a while, you'll consider each of these things automatically.

- **Look for new growth.** By this I mean look for signs that the plant is actively growing. Look at the leaves and stems. There should be signs that the plant is putting on new leaves, and they shouldn't be discolored or malformed. Stems should be firm, not soft. The plant shouldn't look wilted. If those who take care of the plant can't water it, they can't do anything else for it either—this includes preventing insect pests and disease from beginning and spreading. Ask if you can loosen the plant from its pot and observe the roots to see if they're white and plump. You don't want discolored or dark roots. If you see this, put the plant back into its pot and move on. Discolored or dark roots means root rot is beginning,

and soon this will show up in the leaf growth. Remember, if the roots are ever damaged, it'll show up topside in the leaves.

- **Look for insect pests or rot.** Part the leaves and look closely at the plant. You already know the signs and symptoms of insect infestation, and you know that some of these pests are so small that you won't be able to see them. Look for webbing, small moving insects, leaf discoloration, mushy growth, white cottony masses of mealybugs—you know the drill.
- **Look at how the foliage is growing.** You don't want a long stem with leaves beginning one-third of the way up. Look at the leaf nodes (the bumps on the stem from which leaves grow). Does it look as if leaves were once growing there? If so, something is causing leaf drop, and you don't want a sick plant. Sometimes the stems are long but there are no leaf nodes in between a set of leaves. This happens when the plant doesn't get the light it requires. You can tell how long a plant has been sitting on the shelf, out of the light it requires, because there is a good distance between leaf nodes. A short distance means the plant is doing just fine and getting about what it needs. Very little distance means that the plant is getting optimum light requirements and probably just came off the truck (buy it!). You want leaves growing as close to the base of the plant as possible and growing as close to one another as possible.
- **Look at the size of the leaves.** Something's wrong if you see what looks like stunted growth for mature foliage. The plant also should appear properly balanced, not lopsided.
- **Look to see that leaves aren't drooping or curling.** This may indicate that there

is root trouble brewing. Leaves and stems should be firm, strong, and vigorous looking.

- **Look for scorched patches or burned edges on leaves.** Scorched patches may mean that the plant has been given too much fertilizer. And burned leaf edges indicate root damage, overfertilization, or both.

- **Look for flower buds.** If a plant looks as if it's about to bloom, *don't buy it*. Look through the rest of the plants, and find one that's showing some swollen buds or just a little bit of color. Buy that one. You'll enjoy this plant a lot longer if you can watch the buds slowly open in your own home over a period of several days. There's always a chance, too, that the flower bud will drop the minute you get the plant home. Some plants are notorious for this. Christmas cactus *(Schlumbergera bridgesii)* is a prime example. If you think your plant may be one of these, purchase a plant with tight buds that haven't begun to open or show any color. You'll stand a better chance of bringing it into bloom.

- **Look for interesting or pretty leaves on a plant that blooms.** This isn't absolutely necessary, but you might consider it. Look at it this way: Once the plant stops blooming, what's it got going for it to hold your interest? If the plant has interesting or beautiful leaves, it'll continue to add to your enjoyment until it decides to rebloom. Rose growers are going to hate me for this, but it has to be said. This is why I've never taken to growing roses. Yes, the blooms are exquisite. But after they fade, there isn't much left. The plants are unattractive when not in bloom.

Sticks, a few small leaves, and lots of thorns is all I get for my sweat equity and money.

- **Never buy a sick plant no matter how little it costs.** As I always say, *id quod circumiret, circumveniat* (what goes around, comes around).

- **Read the plant tag before you buy.** Make sure that you have the proper environment in your home for the plant to continue to prosper in its new surroundings. Many of the requirements needed to grow the plant will be listed on the tag, which is usually attached to the plant or stuck in the pot. If you can't meet the plant's requirements, don't buy the plant. And don't think you can fool the thing. It knows if it's not being given what it needs, and you'll hear from it as it proceeds to perform poorly.

When to specialize

Your first houseplant choices will be those that interest you, not because of their beauty but because they're easy to care for. Later, when you've gained

Buy a plant in bud, not in flower, so you can enjoy the show.

Plants with interesting foliage like (back to front) arrowhead plant (Syngonium podophyllum), ivy, and polka-dot plant (Hypoestes phyllostachya) can stand on their own and look attractive without flowers.

knowledge on houseplant culture, you'll feel confident enough to try other, more difficult plants. And finally in your development, you'll be attracted to a specific group of plants: cacti, epiphytes, or something all together different. This is the time when you'll use your talent to specialize.

How will you know when it's time to specialize? The decision is usually unconscious. You'll step back from your plant collection one day and notice that it is beginning to lean toward a specific group of plants. You've unconsciously begun to shop for one or two particular groups without realizing it, and they're showing up in your permanent collection without your ever realizing it.

When this happens, you've become a connoisseur of houseplants. And from that point on, not just any plant will do. It must be (for example) a plant of the family *Amaryllidaceae* (the amaryllis family). In order to collect all there is of one family of plants, you'll probably turn to catalogs from mail-order houses specializing in hard-to-find plants. And then you'll actually repeat the process of being a student. You'll learn the cultural requirements of all the plants in this family and become so acquainted with them that you'll know what's possible to grow in your home environment and what's not. The final step in the process will be to artificially change your environmental conditions so that you can grow those few difficult plants anyway and obtain a full collection.

By this time, you've realized that anyone can grow plants to some degree. But to appreciate a particular beauty, form, texture, or growth habit that

catches your fancy is an art. All this time, you've been cultivating these preferences in yourself without realizing it.

I see this same sequence of development taking place in people who first begin an interest in outdoor perennial gardening. After they've learned the culture of plants, they're no longer satisfied with plants that are easy to grow. They want a challenge. They also become enamored of a particular perennial, such as hostas or artemisias. So they collect the hostas that'll grow in their area and then find a plant that won't grow in their area because it's too cold. Now creativity comes into play. If that plant were placed in a sheltered area near a stone wall, it just might survive in the yard. You try it, and voilà! Another triumph! You see how your creative abilities expand and become more in-depth and discerning the more you participate in your interest. And realize this: It's this way with *anything* you attempt.

TIPS

If you summer your plants outdoors, leave the plant tag indoors. I've found that over the course of a few summer months, the lettering on the tag fades and becomes illegible. This happens even when the plants are in the shade. You could, of course, write the plant's botanical name on a store-bought marker and sink this into the pot. And the tag will last longer outdoors if you use indelible black ink.

CHAPTER TEN

TAKING PLANTS OUTSIDE FOR THE SUMMER

S etting houseplants outdoors in the spring is a yearly ritual for many, and I include myself here. When I lived in an apartment, everything went out on the balcony as soon as the night temperatures hit a *consistent* 55°F. I was fortunate because the area never received much full sun. There was always fresh air and shelter from the hard rains and strong winds that came in the spring.

There was a huge sliding glass door opening out onto the balcony. And during the early spring rains (when everything smells so sweet and that damp, earthy smell is a sign the soil is beginning to awaken), I used to slide the door open, sit in front of it, and take in all the smells. The rain obligingly hit the broad wooden railing and splashed onto the leaves of my plants—they loved it. Their nitrogen-rich bath always showed up as new leaf growth.

An all-day spring rain was usually accompanied by a Georges Simenon mystery. I'd catch up with Inspector Maigret, who would be pounding the 1940s Paris streets in the spring rain, and imagine the typical French stone farmhouse set in the countryside, its big clay pots of rosemary and lavender (always spilling over the edges) luxuriating on low stone walls nearby.

Letting Mother Nature take care of your plants for five or six months will improve their appearance. You'll be surprised at what comes back into the house in the fall. Your plants will lose that sickly look, which sometimes results from their having been shut up all winter. The abundance of light, temperature, rain, humidity, and fresh air will work together to rejuvenate plants and create healthier, more robust, lush green foliage.

Here are a few advantages of sending your plants off to summer camp:

• Your plants will increase in size faster if they're kept outdoors.

Your plants love to get out of the house in the summer as much as you do. (Photo by Derek Fell.)

Spring:
moving plants outdoors

- Make sure night temperatures are consistently above 55°F
- Decide which plants should go out
- Decide where each plant should go
- Harden off your plants to the sunlight
- Begin a regular feeding program
- Get rid of any unwanted plants

- Your plants will bloom better.
- Your plants' color will deepen and look more vibrant.
- Rain, which contains nitrogen, will act as a mild fertilizer and will clean the leaves from indoor dust and grime.
- Humidity will make the leaves larger and thicker, and you won't have as many spider mite problems.
- It's easy to repot plants that have outgrown their current quarters and leave them summering outdoors to recuperate before you take them in for the fall.
- It's easier and faster to water with a watering wand outdoors than it is to bring the plants to the sink indoors.
- It's easy to use your hose-end sprayer to fertilize your houseplants when you do all of your other outdoor plants.
- You may be ready for your plants to go: They've been in captivity since you've owned them, but you've *personally* fetched and carried for them all winter; now it's time for them to be on their own for a few months.

When Do They Go Out?

Wait until after the last spring frost date has passed, and then wait an extra two weeks for good measure. Let me give you an example of what I mean.

Here in Tennessee, the last frost date is around April 15. But I always wait until the end of the month to set anything out, just in case we get the unexpected late frost that we never count on. So my plants go out about the first weekend in May. By that time, the night temps aren't low enough to hurt the tender tropicals.

What Should Go Out?

It isn't necessary to put everything outside for the summer. If you do, you may miss having something green inside. You should keep your gesneriads indoors; they and other fuzzy-leaf plants don't like water on their leaves.

The gesneriads belong to a large family of plants (called the *Gesneriaceae*), which includes about 2,000 species. Most members have brightly colored flowers, which aren't like other flowers, and

Because African violets' leaves are sensitive to light, the plants should not be taken outside for the summer. (Photo by Janet Loughrey.)

attractive foliage. Gesneriad flowers are tubular in form. The African violets (*Saintpaulia* species) are about the only ones in this family that produce flowers that look like those of other plants.

Here are some of the genera in the *Gesneriaceae* family that you will want to keep indoors:

• *Achimenes*
• *Aeschynanthus*
• *Columnea*
• *Episcia*
• *Gesneria*
• *Gloxinia*
• *Kohleria*
• *Saintpaulia*
• *Sinningia*
• *Smithiantha*
• *Streptocarpus*

This family is so large that you probably have at least one plant that is a member of it. It would be a good idea to look up your plants in a reference book to see if any of them fall into this huge family.

It may not be wise to put *any* plants outdoors where you live. Industrial metropolises are known for their dirty air, and plants may be better off inside.

And there are certainly plants I can't put outside—they couldn't take it. My peace lily (*Spathiphyllum* 'Mauna Loa'), for example, doesn't go out. It's large, and the leaves can easily burn if the light isn't monitored properly. We also tend to get some strong winds here that could whip the leaves into a ragged mess.

I can't put my ponytail plant (*Beaucarnea recurvata*) out either. It's over 5 ft. tall and the devil to move about. The night-blooming cereus (*Epiphyllum oxypetalum*) also can't go out, because it's a monster, too. And, besides, when the air-conditioner comes on at night, buds begin to set in this plant, which loves a dip in temperature at

The peace lily (*Spathiphyllum* 'Mauna Loa') and ponytail plant (*Beaucarnea recurvata*), which grow into huge plants, should stay indoors year-round.

night. It stays indoors so I can enjoy the perfume and beauty of the flowers.

But there are plants that *must* go out. These are all the amaryllises (*Hippeastrum* species) bulbs that have finished blooming and are ready for their summer out in direct sun, rain, and wind. I have several members of the *Amaryllidaceae* family, and they all want to be outside in the spring. This is one plant that loves as much full sun as it can get in order to build its reserves for the huge blooms it will produce late the next winter.

All my potted herbs that love full sun go out. Years ago, I made little herbal topiary trees (from rosemary and myrtle), which are now quite mature.

Moving an amaryllis outside

This amaryllis has finished blooming and is ready to spend the summer outside.

They only stand 1 ft. to 1½ ft. tall, but they look like nice, thick, little trees (with thick trunks) because they've been pinched back and clipped so much over the years. I set their clay pots on a low stone wall overlooking a perennial bed. There they stand (with the thyme spilling over the wall and at their feet) all summer, soaking up the sun.

The hanging basket plants go out to take their places under the trees or under a shelter so they can get rained on. They are pinched back in the spring, but when they come indoors in the fall, new growth spills out of their baskets and softens the garden room.

If you're a regular visitor to one of the many garden shows in your area each spring (I love these shows), you probably bought several small plants that need to be repotted. Plan to take them out, repot

them, and let them stay outdoors all spring and summer. They'll increase in size so that by fall, you'll take in much larger plants than you bought.

Deciding Where Things Should Go

Give some thought to where you want to summer each of your plants *before* it's time to set them out.

Develop a plan

When I meet with gardening friends in the spring, summering our houseplants is always the topic of discussion over the first spring garden salad. Many friends say they make a diagram that they can follow each year when it comes time to begin this spring task. It saves them having to stand around trying to find a place for everything. As they add a new plant during the year, its position is marked on the diagram.

Most of my friends use a piece of plain white paper and draw their summering areas on it. Then they list the plants they want to put in the area that affords them the best conditions. If plants are to be grouped together, the names are listed in group formation. And because there are always plants that will be added to one's collection and must be fit in here and there, the drawing is usually amended each year.

Know your plants' requirements

Are you familiar with the requirements of each of your houseplants? If not, consult a houseplant directory, and you'll find the light and water requirements you need to help you make your decisions. You also can dig out those plant tags you've set aside as well as any information you've received from mail-order companies. But also use your own good sense. You know how intense the sun is where you live. Just because a plant has been sitting in a south-facing window all winter doesn't mean that it can take the full sun. Most houseplants are tropicals and can't take any full sun—they're jungle plants, remember. Also keep in mind that if you live in the South, the sun is far more intense than it is in the North—southerners will need to keep an eye on their plants to make sure they don't fry.

Summering plants outdoors is particularly hard for apartment dwellers whose space is limited. They haven't much choice. Because of my outdoor space and sheltered areas, I usually take a few plants for the summer to relieve my friends. When these friends get their plants back in the fall, they're always astonished at the growth. One beginner gardener refused a beautiful plant I had given her. She said it couldn't possibly be hers; it didn't look like the small plant she'd given me to care for in the spring. But proof was forthcoming because I knew she was in the habit of initialing the bottom of her clay pots. So I asked her to turn the pot over—her initials were on the bottom.

There is one thing I *won't* do, however. I won't take a friend's prized plant. The fear of accidentally killing it terrifies me. No one knows more about the little idiosyncrasies of plants better than the person who's been taking constant care of them. I know the textbook applications, but plants are a lot like people. Each has its own peculiarities—these are things you can't read in books. You gain this information through experience.

Here's an example. I have a 'Sweet Autumn' clematis (*Clematis paniculata*) that is supposed to bloom in the fall. That's what the books say. It doesn't. It blooms in the late spring every year. Some plants just have a mind of their own.

Outdoor spots for houseplants

Place plants in bright but indirect light so their leaves don't burn. Spots under arbors, awnings, and trees work well.

Here's another example. Do you grow tomatoes? You'll love this one. I like a tomato cultivar called 'Celebrity'. It's supposed to be a determinate tomato; it should grow only a few feet, flower, set fruit, and then die. In my vegetable garden, it climbs out of its 6-ft.-tall, heavy-gauge wire cage (fruiting all the way) and keeps on traveling and fruiting until frost. See what I mean?

In deciding where things ought to go, you may want to keep most of your plants near a watering source. It's so easy each morning simply to reach for the watering wand and flood each pot without having to walk all over the garden to do it. Many people keep plants on sheltered patios where they can be watered easily. Puddles of water can be left standing so plants can enjoy the high humidity that results from these little steam baths throughout the hot summer day.

Make a slow transition

Don't be in a hurry to set things out. Plants need to go through a "hardening off" period of two to three weeks before they're fully acclimated. Hardening off is done in stages, not all at once.

Use yourself as an example. Instead of "hardening off" your skin, you dash outside on the first warm, sunny day. After all, you've been indoors all winter long (six months, more or less). The temp rises to 78°F on a beautiful spring day, and where are you? Working on your tan. But you never realize how intense the sun is, until evening comes. You're as red as a beet. You've blistered tender skin (unused to strong sunlight) without knowing it. The body sheds burned skin because it has become dead cells; the same thing happens to your plants.

Your plants have been inside for six months (more or less), and they've gotten used to less intense, indirect or filtered light coming through a glass pane during the winter. If you set them outdoors on the first sunny day, they'll sunburn and their "skin" will shed, too—their burned leaves will shrivel and fall. They must be moved slowly so their leaves don't burn—they have to be hardened off to intense light just as you do.

Plan to summer your plants out of direct sun anyway—it's far stronger than the sunlight they've been receiving while indoors. Start conditioning your plants to the outdoors by putting them in shaded areas such as under a tree, near overhanging hedges, on umbrella-covered patio tables, or under an arbor or pergola. Over the course of a week or two, gradually move your plants into brighter sunlight. As a rule of thumb, flowering plants prefer bright dappled light, cacti and succulents thrive in slightly stronger light, and foliage plants grow best in light shade with dappled light—no direct sun.

Once you see that your houseplants have acclimated to their surroundings, or hardened off (in about three weeks), and they're obviously arching or bending toward the sunlight, you can move them into a little brighter area.

Give this some thought, too: Once you start setting your plants out, don't set them directly on the soil if you don't intend to plunge them (that is, sink the pots into the ground). Things can come up through the soil or over the pots' rims into the potting soil, and you'll bring these things indoors in the fall. Some people stand their plants on bricks or blocks of decorative wood. Benches, plant stands, tables, and patios are fine, too.

Now That They're Out There, What's Next?

You won't be simply leaving your plants out for the summer to fend for themselves. You need to make sure they get water and food and the right amount of exposure. You also need to make sure pests aren't taking them over. And this is a great time to prune your houseplants to rejuvenate growth and to shape them.

Watering plants

Your plants haven't learned how to scramble down out of their pots and get a drink when they want one. And don't depend on the rain to help—you probably won't get any. Then there's that unexpected wind. It can kick up suddenly, and pots may have to be moved before they topple over and break.

Begin training yourself early on to keep one eye on your plants at all times. All it takes is a few days of bone-dry soil, and parts of your prize rosemary will die. And what's really bad about it is that rosemary (and a few other plants) don't rejuvenate new growth after dying back this way. How would you like to spend two more years retraining your topiary tree back into its previous shape? An ounce of prevention . . .

Begin each day by checking for water needs. I take care of this task bright and early. Because I live in the country, 5:30 A.M. isn't just any 5:30 A.M. It's 5:30 A.M. with the sun rising above a country garden full of country smells. With the birds chirping and singing up a storm, I'm decked out in gardening clothes and water-repellent gardening shoes, a cup of coffee in one hand, a bagel in my mouth, and the hose in the other hand, making my rounds and stopping at each pot.

If you water early in the morning, your plants will have a fighting chance in the heat of the day. This isn't hyperbole. Plants handle heat a lot like we do. We sweat (nongardeners perspire) to lower our body temperature when we get too hot. Plants transpire to lower their temperature when they get too hot. This means that water is brought up from the roots to cool down the leaves. The higher the temperature and lower the humidity, the faster the plant will try to cool itself by transpiring (passing water over its leaves). If it transpires faster than it can get water from the soil, it wilts. And some summer days are so hot that this is just what happens. Even plants in perennial beds wilt at 90°F.

I talked about this earlier in reference to dealing with high temperatures. I said that plants can handle higher temps if more humidity is added. Raising the humidity is like helping the plant transpire—water vapor passes over the leaves. But if the temperature rises and the humidity doesn't, the problem of wilt or collapse begins.

Watering in the morning is better than watering in the evening. Morning watering guarantees that your plants may escape those dreaded fungus attacks. You know what I mean. A night temp of 70°F activates fungi. All they need is the right conditions; and you'll be creating those conditions if you leave your houseplant foliage wet at night. The weather supplies just the right degree of night temperature, you supply the water, and *bingo!* Don't water your plants in the evening. Fungus is not only ugly but also means death to plants.

While we're on the subject of watering: The best device I've seen for watering plants (houseplants and outdoor plants alike) is the long extension wand that screws onto your hose. The stream of water is a gentle, diffused spray, not a raging torrent.

Summer:
care tips

- Check pots every day and water copiously
- Don't forget to water your hanging pots
- Make sure your plants are getting the proper amount of sunlight
- Maintain your feeding program
- Spritz your plants and leave puddles to create humidity
- Make sure that air circulation is good
- Inspect for insect pests often and take appropriate measures to kill them
- Pinch and prune as needed
- Protect your plants from heavy downpours and high winds

A water wand delivers a gentler stream of water than do many other spray attachments.

I've seen people (whom I pretend not to know) water their perennial beds with an unguarded hose. Mud goes everywhere. Soil is splattered all over creation, plants are covered with nastiness, and once-beautiful blooms are face down in the mire. This isn't gardening.

Keep a water-wise eye on your hanging plants. Because they aren't at eye level, hanging pots or baskets may not be remembered when watering time rolls around. We tend not to worry about what we don't see. Remember, though, that warm air rises. And while 6 ft. or so off the ground may not seem high to you, it's hot up there for plants. They're going to dry out a lot faster than if they were at ground level. And hanging clay pots will dry out even faster. These may require watering twice a day.

Become familiar with where you've put all your basket plants. After all you've learned up to this point, you'd kick yourself from here to high noon if something were to die, not from brown

thumb syndrome but from negligence. So after you have put all your plants out, for the first several weeks you may want to set up a temporary routine, as I do. I consult a list of what went where, and I take it with me when I'm out watering.

I learned this lesson the hard way—and I wasn't a beginner when I learned it. I'd finally found the difficult-to-locate glory-bower, or bleeding-heart vine (*Clerodendrum thomsoniae*). It had been a problem to work with and still hadn't settled into the garden room, but I congratulated myself that I was finally beginning to understand its culture and idiosyncrasies. I'd set it in a choice spot away from direct sun and wind where it could catch the rain—then I forgot about it. I happened upon it a few days later. The plant was holding on but wasn't the beauty it had been. In order to conserve water, it had dropped most of its leaves. I had to cut it back, bring it closer to the house, and keep it under a watchful eye for the rest of the summer. The plant is doing fine now, but I almost lost it. It took an entire growing season for my plant to recover.

Feeding plants

Don't forget to feed your plants occasionally, too. Remember, summer is their growing season. They'll need food in order to continue putting on new growth. I feed all my plants with a quarter-strength water-soluble plant food every week. Does this sound like a lot of food? It's not—for the hot summer.

Food is leached from pots at a faster rate when they're outside, because the plants are watered so often either by me or by the rains. Some clay pots are watered twice a day. What food is left is all that the growing plant gets. So I step up feeding in the summer—but only quarter-strength weekly feedings. They'll also get some nitrogen from the rain to help them along the way.

Once a month, I like to feed everything with fish fertilizer. It's natural, it breaks up the chemical food cycle, and it's mild. It also stinks. This is another reason why I like to use it outdoors. Plants love it.

Plunging pots

Plunging (sinking the pots into the ground) was done more in the 1940s and 1950s than it is today. And it was certainly done centuries earlier. I think it's rarely done today because people just have far too many other calls upon their free time and can't be bothered with it. Today, the closest we come to plunging is setting plants under trees or beneath overhanging shrubs. Pots don't make it into the ground much anymore. And not all plants can be plunged. Delicate plants should be placed in sheltered areas or kept inside altogether because they can't take the rigors that Mother Nature offers up each spring and summer.

There are several reasons why pots are plunged.

What's in them won't escape Are you an herb lover who simply must grow mint? Then you'll need to cage it. You should keep it confined in pots, and sink the pots into the ground. But leave 2 in. of rim showing aboveground. Your mint won't dry out as fast, and (in my opinion) the mint will prosper better than if you left it topside sitting on your patio. It's also less likely to grow rampant in the garden. If you don't want it everywhere, then you should keep it in pots. Even then, it'll try to outsmart you by crawling out the drainage hole at the bottom of its pot. Mint can tunnel underground 6 in. down, only to resurface and continue to spread. For this reason, use a deep pot to cage it. But watch out, it may lie down on the ground, root itself again (just to be on the safe side and to cause you further grief), and continue traveling.

What's in them can be quickly removed from the soil When you want to bring the plant inside for the fall, all you have to do is take the pot out of the ground. You'll clean it up a little, and take it in. How is this different from keeping the pot on the patio? Things planted in the ground get to take advantage of all those good things that help plants—like worm castings, which are better fertilizer than anything that comes out of a container.

What's in them won't have to be repotted in the fall The plant is already in its pot when you extract it from the soil, so there's no need to repot—not in the fall anyway. It's better to repot in the spring when the plant's actively growing and the roots can fill the new pot without rotting. In the fall, the plant's ready to rest, to go dormant. It won't grow or fill up a new pot with roots; the excess space in a larger pot means damp soil and too much moisture around the roots, which will eventually cause root rot.

What's in them can get rained on easily I've noticed that just because a plant is on the patio doesn't mean it'll get rained on that much. But if it's in the soil, it picks up the moisture from the surrounding area—especially if it's in a clay pot.

What's in them won't tip over It's easy for plants to topple over in a strong wind. We have those winds where I live, and I'm forever having to keep watch to make sure that pots are anchored before one of our summer gully washers comes. I use a lot of clay pots, and one reason is because they don't tip over easily.

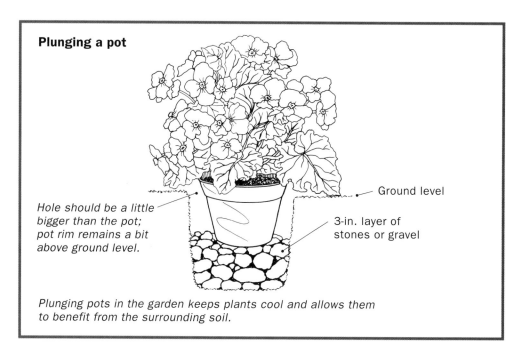

Plunging a pot

Hole should be a little bigger than the pot; pot rim remains a bit above ground level.

Ground level

3-in. layer of stones or gravel

Plunging pots in the garden keeps plants cool and allows them to benefit from the surrounding soil.

Every spring, I plunge my amaryllis pots in an area of full sun after they've all bloomed. I pot them up three to five amaryllis bulbs to a pot, making sure that each group is the same color. Then when they finally do bloom in the early spring (February and March), they make quite a big show.

But not all plants should be plunged in full sun. The foliage of some bulbs must have as much sun as possible, but tropicals and most other houseplants shouldn't. These plants are used to growing in rain forests under a canopy of trees, not under a full solar blast. Always be familiar with your plants' light requirements before putting them in direct sun.

If you'd like to try your hand at plunging, here's how:

1. Dig a hole a little larger than the pot. Long ago, a whole bed was dug for the potted plants, and they were all set in together and plunged. But this task may prove a bit too bothersome today. Chances are you have only a few plants to plunge, so individual holes work fine.

2. Fill the bottom of the hole with a 3-in. layer of stones or gravel. This will prevent worms and other creepy-crawlies from going up through the drainage hole and into the pot.

3. Set the pot in the hole a little above ground level. Backfill the hole, placing soil around the pot.

4. Each week, turn the pot. This will prevent the roots from anchoring into the soil below the pot. If this happens, it's difficult to remove the pot from the soil in the fall. You'll also want to turn the pot so that each side of the plant can develop in a uniform fashion. The pot stays in its hole all spring and summer as part of the landscape, enjoying the bright dappled sunlight, invigorating rains, fresh air, and humidity.

5. In the fall, dig up the pot. Clean it off and return it to the indoors.

Double-potting for moisture

If you're on the go in the summer and don't have time to water, double-potting may be the thing for you. Double-potting involves putting your plant (pot and all) into another pot that's bigger and stuffing the space between the two pots with wet long-fiber sphagnum moss (see Chapter 2 for details). The idea is that the sphagnum moss will keep the pot from drying out so fast in the heat. When you water your plant, you'll also water the sphagnum moss, which will hold the water for a long time. Long-fiber sphagnum moss is easy to work with and can be found at any garden center. I don't use this method because I am able to tend my plants every day, but it might be just the thing for you.

Dealing with pests

Throughout the spring and summer, check your plants often for insect pests. Since your houseplants are out in nature now, pests are more prevalent. And once they get started, they move in to take over and weaken one plant after another. When dealing with insect pests, prevention should be your aim.

I've already given you extensive advice on handling insect pests (see Chapter 8), but here's a quick, on-the-spot way you can get rid of any insect pests you see on your plants while you're carrying out your daily watering tasks.

Turn the hose on them. By summer, the water coming through my hose is fairly warm. So I hose down my plants at least once a week with a strong, fine spray. This dislodges pests and knocks them off the plants. Doing this once a week will ensure that pests don't set up housekeeping and begin an infestation.

But, as you can probably guess by now, there is another reason that I like to hose the plants down. The water raises the humidity around the plants. Remember what I said about high temperatures. Plants don't like hot temps (anything over 75°F) unless air movement and/or humidity are added.

Well, you needn't worry about air movement, because the plants are outside and usually whipped about by constant breezes, but it also would be beneficial if you would raise the humidity. This is particularly important if you live in a hot, dry climate. Hose down the area around the plants after you finish knocking the bugs off. Leave puddles of standing water wherever you can so that throughout the hot days, your plants can take a reviving steam bath and feel refreshed—they may feel the heat, but the humidity will allow them to deal with it.

Pinching and pruning

During the course of the winter months, plants get lanky or produce spindly growth so that the overall effect is rather sparse. You'll want to stimulate new growth so that the result is a compact, more bushy appearance.

The procedure for creating bushy plants is known as pinching, and the procedure for shaping plants is called pruning. Spring is the best time to pinch and prune plants because they'll put their foliage back on faster during this active growth period. The result will be a bushier plant to bring indoors for the fall.

If I double-pot my plants when I set them out for the summer, should I remove the sphagnum packing between the pots before bringing the plants in for the fall?

Yes. You don't want your plants to hold water for long periods during the winter—rot will result. Double-potting is used in the summer months to keep plants moist.

Through specialized pruning, this azalea has taken the form of a tree, called a standard. (Photo by Karen Bussolini.)

Can you give me an example of pinching in flowering plants?

Have you seen the popular blue fanflower *(Scaevola aemula)*? This is a gorgeous trailing houseplant and is one you'll want because of its flowers and because you can leave it outside until temperatures dip to 28°F in the fall.

The blue fan-shaped flowers appear off the tips of the plant's stems. This plant is a fast grower (it'll grow 2 ft. in six weeks), and fast growers can get lanky and sparse before long, so keep it thick and bushy by pinching. When the flowers die, pinch the tip ends off, and side shoots will grow from either side of the stem—you'll have two new stems in place of one. As these get longer, pinch them, and you'll have two more. The more stems you have, the more flowers you'll have.

If you want to keep your geraniums bushy and full of colorful blooms, pinch them, too.

What you do   Pinching involves using the forefinger and thumbnail to pinch out soft stem growth immediately above the leaf node—the point where the leaf is attached to the stem. Pinching is done on the soft tip growth (the very end) of a stem of flowers, foliage, or herbs. It causes more stems to form and thus more flowers or foliage.

Pruning is usually done to woody growth, like that on shrubs, trees, and shrubby houseplants. Pruning cuts are made either along a stem or flush with the main limb, either to get rid of unwanted limbs altogether or to "head back" the plant. *Heading back* means that new growth will come below the cut all along the stem or branch, not just at the tip. For shrubby plants and trees, this works like pinching does and keeps plants nice and bushy. Pruning also may be done for houseplants that need shaping and training.

The result   When you pinch or prune just above a set of leaves, new stems will branch out from either side of that point. Pinch those when they get a little bigger, and you'll have even more stems. If you pinch or prune a flowering plant, you'll have more flowers because you've stimulated the plant to make more stems. This is how the plant rejuvenates its growth if, for some reason, some of the outer leaves or stems have been damaged. But a plant will not volunteer to branch on its own. There is a hormone at the tips of the outer leaves of most plants that prevents branching. If this hormone is removed by pinching or pruning, the outer tip growth begins to branch. Plants (like people) will not volunteer to do anything they don't have to do.

Here is an example of pruning to get more flowers. Do you have an azalea as a houseplant? It's probably a florist azalea *(Rhododendron indica),* which can be made into a "standard." This does well as a houseplant. You'll want it to stay bushy so that when it flowers again, it'll be covered in blooms. This means you'll have to prune. When your plant finishes flowering, prune the old flowers at the stem. In a few weeks, you'll see new growth beginning. Don't prune early azaleas at all after May or June because they'll have started setting their flowering buds for next year's bloom, and you don't want to cut them off.

Woody houseplants, such as gardenias, citruses, and fuchsias, particularly benefit from pruning, but there are also many others you can prune.

The best time to prune (or train) a plant so that it will grow into a specific shape is when it's young. Sometimes you learn this the hard way.

I had been working with rosemary early in my houseplant experience. I wanted to make a rosemary tree (the

Pinching back a plant

Pinching back the growing tip on many plants encourages branching, which keeps the plant compact and healthy.

Split-leaf philodendron (*Monstera deliciosa*) can be pinched to create a full and bushy plant. (Photo by Janet Loughrey.)

process is called "topiary"). Instead of continually pruning when the plant was young, I slipped up a few times and forgot to do it. The result was that I had to cut off a lot of mature growth and take the plant back to the point where I should have made my pruning cuts earlier. The experience taught me to shape and train *early,* as the plant begins to mature.

Did you know that you can increase your herb foliage without planting new plants? You do this by pinching. When you pinch herbs, the plants look bushier and grow even more leaves. Do your first pinching when the herb is no more than 6 in. tall. From then on, it will continue to branch as it grows. Continue to pinch every three to four weeks. Have you ever wondered how nurseries get herbs like rosemary, thyme, and lavender to bush out and make such full growth? They do the same thing you're doing—they pinch back all the growing tips. This applies not only to the herbs you grow in your

garden but also to those you grow in pots. Try pinching rosemary, lavender, basil, thyme, hyssop, and other herbs. Your plants will increase in size and beauty, and you'll have more leaves to use in cooking and crafts.

You even can pinch some vegetable garden plants. Do you grow hot or sweet bell peppers? After you plant your 6-in. transplants in the garden, pinch the stem at the tip and they'll branch—you'll have more peppers. If you pinch the tips of all the side shoots every three weeks, you'll have even more. I do this if I have room only for a few plants. I end up getting as many peppers from branching fruit as I would if I had increased the number of plants.

Some foliage plants can be pinched, but others can't. Foliage plants such as *Spathiphyllum, Sansevieria,* bromeliads, *Aspidistra,* palms, *Aglaonema,* dracaenas, *Dieffenbachia,* and African violets can't be pinched because their growth comes directly from the soil or from crowns. But *Monstera, Brugmansia,* philodendrons, coleuses, pothos, *Tradescantia,* and other soft-stemmed plants can be pinched; their growth is on stems.

Watch what you're doing whenever you pinch or prune. Be mindful that you're not taking away from only one side of the plant and creating a lopsided effect. Stop what you're doing, step back, and look at the plant. If one side looks fuller, take growth from the other side. Pinching and pruning should result in a symmetrical-looking plant.

Don't use leaf polishes

People like to see the shiny new growth on plants and think that the growth will always stay shiny. It won't. Shiny new leaves are like a baby's skin—fresh, new, and vibrant. But as the baby and the leaves grow, they both age—the fresh, new look is left behind. Learn to accept the plant as it is, with all its blemishes and age marks. You can't improve on Mother Nature. If you must have shiny leaves, buy plastic plants.

Leaf polishes clog the pores on the leaf surface just like dust and dirt. For your plant's continued good health, omit polishes and keep the tops and undersides of the leaves clean.

Get rid of what you don't like

Spring is a good time to clean house, so to speak. Which plants didn't make it over the winter and are just hanging on? Which plants gave you continual trouble and are just languishing in their pots? Which plants are eyesores, more like twigs stuck in the soil than houseplants in healthy condition?

Weed out your collection. Consider whether you should keep certain plants. By the end of the summer, you'll go through this process again—it's continual. You're striving for excellence, not mediocrity, as a houseplant gardener. Good taste and an eye for beauty are learned—you aren't born with a discriminating eye; it must be cultivated. Learn what looks good, what's worth the time and space to keep, and what's not.

Never keep a plant out of guilt or sympathy. If you hate it, you hate it. Every time you look at your collection, you'll see that plant as a constant reminder of how much better looking the whole collection would be without it. Get rid of it. What should you do with your unwanted plant?

- Give it to another beginner.
- Give it to a garden center.
- Give it to a friend who needs cheering up.
- Give it to a plant society to sell.
- Give it to a child interested in learning about houseplants.
- Sell it at a yard sale.
- Organize a houseplant sale with friends and hope someone buys it.
- Take it to the hospital and leave it at the nurses' station for them to enjoy.
- Swap with a friend for a plant you do like.
- Put it in a pretty basket with an attractive bow, tuck in a favorite gardening magazine, and take it to a gardening friend recovering from a hospital stay.

If all else fails, bury the plant in the compost pile. Out of sight, out of mind. At least it will go out with a purpose—nourishing other plants down the road.

CHAPTER ELEVEN

BRINGING PLANTS INDOORS FOR THE WINTER

Summer's over. Most of the flowering perennials in your outdoor garden have already spent themselves. The nights are getting noticeably cooler. And around the house, you're preparing for the fall season—*and so are your plants.*

Plants must go through their usual dormancy period (a resting cycle) of a few months before they become active again. Your blooming plants especially will need a quiet time—it takes a lot of energy to produce those flowers. But almost all plants have a dormancy cycle of one fashion or another. Your outdoor perennials retreat underground (where they still remain a little active in warmer winters like mine) from heavy frosts and snow, and the vines on your arbor look like lifeless masses of twisted brown cord. The trees in your backyard drop their leaves and go dormant. Inside, your ferns are quiet, the cacti just sit there, and some flowering plants, such as vintage cyclamens, look as if they're dying. From fall until spring, your houseplants won't grow much or put on many new leaves. They're simply in a holding pattern.

It's time to start thinking about bringing in your houseplants.

"I Didn't Realize I Had So Many Plants!"

If you're like me, over the summer you acquired a few new plants that you just had to have (you didn't know where you'd put them, but you had to have them), and now the unavoidable moment has come to decide where you'll put the plants once you have brought them inside.

You stand there sipping coffee under the arbor. In front of you is a sizable (and impressive) green array—beautiful, luxuriant, and healthy. You can't wait to bring in all your plants and show them off during the winter to visitors who want to drop by and see the plant room. As you stand back, you try to get an overall view of what you have. In your mind you separate the sun lovers from the low-light lovers. The plants that need the most sun will have to go close to the south- or west-facing windows. And the low-light plants can take up positions away from the window.

Plants that summer outside make a lush windowsill display during the winter. (Photo by Karen Bussolini.)

I don't know about you, but when fall comes, I start thinking about bringing greenery indoors anyway. I know where these thoughts come from. All the flowers in the garden are played out, the perennials have been divided, leaves have been shredded and worked into the beds for next spring, and the vegetable garden has had a hundred or so bags of leaves tilled into the soil. In the midst of all the duties requiring the handling of dead and decayed material, I begin to want something living and green to get me through the cold, gray months ahead.

"But where did I ever get all of these plants?" is always the question I end up asking myself. Just as Sherlock Holmes had his three-pipe problem, I have my three-cup dilemma. There's a lot of coffee drinking around my house in the fall.

Helping Plants Adjust

Before you turn on the heat for winter, you'll have to take your plants through a brief transition period. This consists of getting them inside and situated into their winter positions so that they're used to being indoors with less sunlight, less humidity, and less air circulation.

Some plants rebel and show annoyance at too quick a change, so ease them into a new situation. The weeping fig *(Ficus benjamina)* is a prime example of this. Stand it outside all summer so that it gets a few hours of morning sun, fresh air, ample water, and high humidity, and it will put on a thick set of leaves. The thing's beautiful by the time fall rolls around. And it looks the way a tree is supposed to look. But bring it back inside, and you know what happens. It throws a fit—literally throws off its leaves in irritation at having been moved out of its prime location.

It'll put on another set of leaves, certainly, but they'll be much thinner and smaller—and better able to deal with indoor conditions. You'll have to wait for months before the plant gets back to normal. Meanwhile, you must endure the daily heartbreak of scooping up handfuls of yellowed leaves from the carpet.

How can you make the transition an easy one so that plants moving back indoors don't throw a tantrum? Think back to what you did in the spring when you were setting your plants outdoors. You moved them into their summer places little by little. You didn't put sun lovers into full sun right away. They were gradually moved; and even then, they were never put into direct full sun. This is what you'll have to do in the fall. A gradual move will cut down on falling leaves and other signs of disapproval.

Here in Tennessee, I begin preparing my plants in early September by inching them away from high light levels and humidity. My friend Joy, an experienced houseplant gardener, hasn't much room for the inching process, so she gradually drops a shade cloth down the front of her pergola, where her plants are summered. This lowers light levels beautifully.

Starting this early allows plants to adjust to the lower light levels in your house. This is the *most important* factor of all the adjustments they'll have to make. The thing that helps you out is that plants are already beginning to slow down their growth, which means that their light requirements won't be as great.

But you'll also have to get your plants acclimated to the big drop in humidity they'll experience indoors, and this is the *second most important* adjustment they must make. The humidity is already low indoors, and it will be even lower when the furnace kicks in. But you can handle this, too. You have a secret weapon to deal with this problem—your steam vapor humidifier.

If you can handle these two factors (diminished light and lower humidity), the adjustment period will take place without your plants' being aware of the changes. When it comes time to move things indoors, the sun lovers will be ready to take lower light and decreased humidity because you've prepared them—there won't be any surprises. Plants that don't require high levels of light won't be bothered at all by the trip back inside.

Step-by-Step Guide to Moving Plants Indoors

Here are steps to follow that will help you organize the fall migration indoors. Simply do each step in the order I've given them to you. This method will save you time and sweat equity.

1. Reduce the light and humidity requirements

Four to six weeks before nighttime temps are likely to dip below 55°F in your area, begin moving your plants away from the light and decrease the humidity around them. Every few days, inch them back a little more. Also decrease the humidity around the plants by keeping the patio dry of puddles and standing water. This period will allow you time to complete Step 2.

After adjusting for four to six weeks, they'll be ready to take the diminished indoor conditions. But by that time you will have improved those conditions by turning on the ceiling fans to increase air circulation, bringing out the humidifier to provide them with much-needed humidity, and shifting them closer to the light source. Remember, the plants have been living in the best of conditions for

five or six months, and now they must adapt to new conditions. It will take some time for them to adjust.

2. Make a plan

After you start the inching process, plan where things will go indoors. I draw a plan on paper and label where each plant goes. Then by the time I bring the plants in, I don't waste time standing around holding pots and trying to get light exposures right for each one. I also save the plan for the next fall, making additions for newcomers to my collection.

3. Go over each pot carefully

There are a variety of mini-steps necessary at this time. Don't skip any. Time spent now will pay off later.

Remove any dead or decaying leaves
Dead or decaying organic material is an invitation to bacteria to move in and

Fall:
moving plants indoors

- Begin four to six weeks before nighttime temperatures drop below 55°F
- Inch plants away from strong sunlight
- Decide where each plant should go
- Go over each pot carefully
- Water your plants before bringing them inside
- Stop your feeding program
- Get rid of any unwanted plants
- Keep the indoor humidity up

finish the process. When you remove decaying leaves and flowers from the area around the plant, you also remove any insect pests hiding there—insect pests that could cause you trouble if they're taken inside.

Decaying plant material also has an odor. Some of it is sweet, like a leaf pile left to decompose for later use in the garden. But there is also the nasty smell that comes with other kinds of decay. And this isn't what you want in your home—especially since you're about to close it up for the winter.

Finally, decaying material just looks bad. You'll want a tidy, pleasing collection of plants to display during the holiday season. People will be in and out looking at your collection. What impression do you want to leave with them?

Remove spent flowers When a plant that is in the process of flowering comes back into the house after having had perfect

Removing flowers

Help ease your plant's adjustment to indoor life by removing any spent flowers.

growing conditions outside, it doesn't do well. The plant must turn its attention to adjusting to the indoors. Maintaining its flowers will only weaken it. Help the plant conserve its energy for the long winter months ahead: Cut off the flowers.

Try to avoid pruning or pinching You want your plants to look full and vigorous for the winter; that's part of their jungly appeal. If you pinch or prune now, no new growth will occur. Remember, the plant is going into its resting cycle. It doesn't grow when it's resting. Whenever possible, leave your plants full with the growth you worked to encourage last spring.

Don't repot Repotting should be left for spring. If you repot now, you'll disturb the plant's roots when it's about to rest. Leave it alone. Plants do better in smaller pots over the winter anyway—there's less chance of rot.

If you shift up into a larger pot, you'll be adding more soil. This means there's more soil to stay damp for longer periods of time and more chance for root rot. Remember, too, that fresh potting soil has some fertilizer in it—enough for two months. Plants can't use fertilizer if they aren't growing. Save your soil and effort for the spring when the plant is just waking up and ready to put on some active growth.

The only *exceptions* to repotting are amaryllises. If you've plunged their pots out in the garden during the summer, all you have to do is dig them up, wash off the pots, and cut their foliage back. If you planted them directly into the garden, you'll have to repot them. Choose a clean pot, crock it, and add some fresh potting soil. Lift the bulbs from the garden, and repot them so that half the bulb sticks out of the pot. Then cut back the foliage and bring the plant into the house. Don't water amaryllises after the last weekend in August. Force them into an early rest by keeping them dry and cool (no lower than 40°F) in an unheated room, and you'll have your buds peeking out in three months.

Don't apply leaf polish If you want plastic plants, buy them; don't use leaf polish. Real plants don't have shiny leaves all the time. Only new leaves are shiny. Plants don't look natural when they're as shiny as a pair of new shoes. As a leaf ages, it grows dull in color.

Leaf polish also adds a coating to the leaf that isn't natural. Pores (stomata) in the leaf need to stay clean. The plant has enough difficulty maintaining a homeostatic balance of water, air, and light without your adding chemicals to the mix and clogging its pores.

Look for insect pests Look for webbing between the stem and leaves or on the undersides of leaves. Look for any creepy-crawlies in the soil, too. You don't want them coming in with you for the winter. Worms love to climb into my pots. And they always end up crawling out and into the garden room.

To prevent this, you may want to gently unpot your small plants, being careful to keep the soil intact around the root ball. You might be able to spot a few worms and get rid of them. Toss them back into your garden if you have one. Their castings are high in nitrogen and good for plants.

If worms are so good for plants, why don't you want to keep them in your pots? Because worms move out of any soil that's water-logged. So once you water your plants thoroughly, the worms will exit the pots anyway. They can't fertilize plants they aren't near.

Looking for stowaway pests

Pull a plant out of its pot so you can spot any pests easily.

Some early houseplant writers (present-day ones, too, I suspect) advocated a systemic pest treatment for the soil when plants were being prepared for the indoors. I don't care for this because it could make you lazy about looking out for pests. Showers twice a month (in the tub) and a little soaping will take care of most problems. I also don't like the use of systemics, because you never know who might eat the soil or the plants—your baby or your pet.

Look carefully through your hanging plants Your hanging baskets have been up and out of eye-level sight for months. Don't bring them in before checking to see if small birds or frogs have taken up residence. This happens often in the country. You may even have a late nesting—a mama still feeding her babies. I get birds occasionally, and I'm forever bringing in little tree frogs, which croak all night long until I manage to locate them and put them outside.

I've even known gardeners to take large baskets down only to find snakes in them. Snakes *do* climb up into shrubs and small trees here (I've seen them on our property), so I wasn't surprised when I heard this—but one gardener was. I'm told it took her more than an hour to recover from the shock.

Snakes can be persuaded easily to move on. Just set the pot on the ground and the creature will exit by itself. If it insists on squatter's rights, use a long pole or stick—*step back some distance*—to edge it along out of the pot. If the snake accepts the challenge and comes toward you, don't stick around to charge it rent. Call the animal control service in your area; they know how to take over.

I've come face to face with green garden snakes that have crawled up in the hedges in the evening. Not an enjoyable experience. I know they're beneficial, but they give me the willies, and it's a shock when they come upon you unexpectedly. They blend in so well that you don't notice them until they begin to move or your eyes see them for what they are.

Gently hose off and spray plants At this point, I like to work from a patio table. I use a pump-up sprayer and spray either the Old Soap Bath Remedy (see p. 84) or the All-Purpose Insect Spray (see p. 84) to control insect pests. I prefer the pump-up sprayer because I have so many plants, and the canister holds 2 gallons of finished spray. These remedies work wonders in removing insect pests.

A word of warning: Be sure that you're familiar with your plants to the extent that you know which ones don't mind the soap treatment and which ones do.

Soap baths won't remove insects completely because there still may be eggs on the undersides of leaves. But the solution will dry their little hides out or make them sick. I always respray plants two or three days later in order to kill any recent hatchlings.

Staying out all spring and summer, plants pick up a lot of insects, and for this reason, some garden writers are against sending houseplants out into nature—they would rather see them stay indoors. Their main idea is that houseplants are houseplants—not outdoor plants. You'll have to decide this one for yourself. These writers also don't believe that it's worth all the trouble to lug them outdoors, water and care for them in the summer, pestproof them in the fall, and lug them back inside.

My feeling about the matter is that plants benefit greatly from being in the fresh air, being rained upon, and being placed in better light than is available indoors. There's just too much to be gained by setting plants outdoors—and they look magnificent by fall.

Clean the outside of each pot This is for looks more than anything. Rain splashes nastiness all over pots and dirties them up by the end of the season. A little soap spray and rubbing will set everything right again. And while you're at it, make sure the drainage hole is unclogged.

Water your plants Give each pot a good drink of water before bringing it inside. The only exception is your potted amaryllis; don't water it for the next three months—it must rest dry. Watering your collection now will spare you having to do it later after the plants are in and you're worn out.

Don't feed the plants Since plants don't actively grow in the fall and winter, they don't use food. The fertilizer just sits in the soil, creating a fertilizer salt problem.

Here's my rule of thumb: Houseplants shouldn't receive any food from the first weekend in August to March. Resume feeding when you see them putting on some new spring growth. The exception again is the amaryllis. After it blooms, begin feeding it. That kind of flower production needs some food behind it.

4. Bring each pot indoors
Arrange each plant according to its light requirement. If a plant has had strong light or some direct sun outside, move it closer to the window inside. This light business is another reason that some people think it's unwise to summer plants outdoor. They feel that plants get used to their indoor environment and should remain there, and that moving them in and out only stresses them.

They also believe that those living in cities should think twice about moving plants outdoors because of the smog and filthy air they'd exist in. I'm sure their concerns about the smog are well founded. So the best advice here would be for city dwellers to consider their options and weigh the situation. Your indoor environment may be the cleanest place to grow your plants.

This is also a good time to decide if you really want to use up precious indoor space for a plant that didn't do well during the summer. If in doubt, throw it out or give it to a friend.

5. Keep the humidity up
Plants have just come indoors after having been outside in high humidity (depending on the part of the country you're in) all summer. Take them out of it immediately, and you can expect trouble. Using a steam humidifier may prevent the leaves of sun lovers from turning yellow and dropping. Turn on your humidifier near your plants for 8 to 10

Indoor spots for houseplants

Remember to place plants where their light and humidity needs will be met. Don't put low-light plants near a south window, and don't put flowering plants in the center of a room with a north window.

hours a day, but never let the hot steam touch any foliage.

You'll want to turn on the heat anyway during those early chilly days, and a humidifier will raise the temperature in the room. As the saying goes, it's not the heat, it's the humidity. Humidity increases air temperature, so you might not have to depend on the furnace quite so much.

If you don't want to use a humidifier, try misting or some of the other tricks discussed in Chapter 5.

Winter Care Notes
In the winter when plants are dormant, they don't need much. Your major

Can I pot up plants in the garden and bring them indoors to enjoy for the winter?

Yes. Some people like to bring in daisies and small dahlias. You may also want to bring in herbs from your herb garden. I pot up lavender and rosemary. Chives do well in a kitchen window, and so do garlic, rosemary, and thyme. Sage and basil may have gotten a bit too big to move.

Here's how to do it:

1. Dig your plants, trying to get as much of the root ball as possible.

2. Get a clean pot (clay is best) and use your best potting soil.

3. Water the plant after you pot it up.

There are all kinds of windowsill herb-growing kits on the market now, and they include the herbs that grow best under windowsill conditions. You might try one of these.

concerns will be to keep the humidity up to 55 to 60 percent, maintain the air circulation, and prevent insect pest invasions. Your plants will be in a holding pattern until February or March, when they will begin their growth cycle again. But for now, they need less water, warmth, and light (not as much as in summer when they're actively growing), and no food. Winter care will be less demanding for you at this point, and you'll be able to enjoy your plants more. Here are a few things to keep in mind.

Water

Since most plants aren't actively growing in the winter, they need less water. They will stay moister for longer periods of time. This saves you a lot of hauling pots or water back and forth.

In the winter, I always handle watering this way: When the plants are taken to the shower once or twice a month for their soap bath (to discourage insect pests), I let them get good and soaked. This is because I use clay pots, and the pots and soil dry out faster than they would if I'd potted plants in plastic ones.

I like clay pots as a protection against overwatering, especially in the winter. Clay insures no chance of overwatering. If you're a plastic person and don't like clay pots at all, you could slip a few of your more difficult plants (those you know are more subject to root and crown rot) into clay pots for the winter and then put them back into their plastic pots in the spring. They aren't going to put on much root growth during the winter, so they ought to go back into their plastic pots nicely without putting up a fight.

If you bring your rosemary, lavender, chives, and other herbs indoors, keep them in clay pots that are about the same size as the plant's root ball. Most of these herbs come from regions of the world

where they get excellent drainage and stay dry for long periods. In small clay pots, they won't keep their feet wet all the time, and you'll be less likely to lose them to rot. Also, *don't* fertilize your herbs at any time, because their essential oils will be less potent if you treat them this well. They simply aren't used to it. Keep them in bright light, and clip them whenever you need a few leaves for the soup pot.

Temperature

In addition to less water, resting plants need less warmth. As a matter of fact, some plants that flower in the fall or winter won't set bloom until the temperature drops.

My clivia (*Clivia miniata*) and I used to have it round and round about its blooming habit. Clivias won't set bud until they've been through a dry period and the temp dips to about 50°F. If the temperature rises above 50°F, they refuse to send up their bloom stalk. The blooms stay down in between the leaves and peek out—they won't rise above the plant as they're supposed to.

Christmas cactus (*Schlumbergera bridgesii)* is easy. I just leave it outside until it's been in temperatures of 40° to 50°F at night for several weeks, and then I slowly move it indoors into a cool room where I can enjoy it. If the room is too warm, it'll say so by dropping all of its buds. *Epiphyllum* cacti like to be treated the same way.

The opposite is true with amaryllis bulbs. If they've been staying at 40°F for three months, they're ready to bloom—their rest is finished. Bring them to the kitchen sink and water them well with warm water. Keep them in a warm room, and the bloom stalk will appear one to four weeks later.

Are you forcing other bulbs, such as tulips or daffodils, in pots? They, too, need to go through a cold period of three months (at 40°F) in order to form their roots. Then you can water them; stand back, though— they'll practically leap out of the pots.

Light and humidity

Some gardening books advocate cutting back all plants that are brought into the house for fall. These writers believe that when the robust growth is brought back inside, the plants will drop all of their leaves. This, they say, is due to the difference in light levels. Plants simply can't use the thick, large leaves they put on outdoors to gather sunlight when they come back indoors, so they shed these and grow smaller, thinner leaves. In this way, the plant is thought to acclimate itself to indoor light levels.

Wait a minute! You didn't put your plants into high light levels outside. You shaded them and, at most, gave your tropicals bright light but not direct sun. Your plants have larger leaves because of the increased humidity they luxuriated in while they were outside—not because they were placed in a sunny area. After all, the leaves of jungle plants (the same ones you grow at home) are sheltered by a thick canopy of trees overhead—they don't get much sun. But they *do* get high humidity. And now you can deal with the situation. Don't move your plant closer to the window; break out the humidifier.

When you bring your plants indoors during their fall acclimating period, increase the humidity by using your steam humidifier. You shouldn't get much, if any, leaf drop. You'll have to use the humidifier anyway when the furnace comes on, so you might as well do it now. Leaf drop needn't happen if you're careful about the humidity.

Winter:
care tips

- Water only when the plants need watering
- Don't forget to water your hanging pots
- Make sure your plants are getting the proper amount of sunlight
- Do not feed plants during their resting cycle
- Maintain indoor humidity at 55 to 60 percent in the plants' immediate area
- Make sure air circulation is good
- Keep the daytime temp around 70°F and let the nighttime temp drop to 60°F
- Inspect for insect pests often, and take appropriate measures to kill them

Air circulation

If you have a ceiling fan in the plant room, turn it on when the plants are inside. You never want still air in your plant room no matter what time of the year it is. Ceiling fans will keep the air moving, help prevent fungus, and keep the temperature comfortably low.

The fan may even help your plants to set buds. I discovered this with my night-blooming cereus *(Epiphyllum oxypetalum)* in the fall and winter (I also get buds in the spring). The minute the ceiling fan goes on, the plant starts putting on buds all over, and soon I have an explosion of exquisite blossoms that are larger than the spread of my palm and fingers. The same thing happens with the *Clivia miniata,* which is not easy

Clivia (Clivia miniata) is heralded as one of the easiest houseplants to grow, but it won't bloom until it experiences cool night temperatures. (Photo by Erik Simmons.)

to bring into bloom. I suspect that the plant room is a little too warm for these plants when the fan isn't cooling the air to a good budding temperature. The plants bloom at the same time. And one time my large pot of *Clivia miniata* sent up two bloom stalks—one from an old plant and one from a two-year-old offset that had not been separated from the adult.

Insect pest prevention

Prevention is the key word here. This is because pests must not be allowed to establish themselves. Once they do, they'll ravage a collection in no time. I've seen garden rooms so overcome by whiteflies that clouds of them were

everywhere. Insects reproduce fast, in days in most instances. And if you're using the grouping method of displaying and increasing humidity around your plants, pests can travel even faster from plant to plant.

For this reason, soap showers and other remedies are imperative. Spider mites, the most dreaded of all houseplant pests, *hate* moisture. But don't wait until you see pests before you do something about them. Prevention, remember? I've always noticed that whenever I wash the leaves of tropical plants once a month with a soap spray and use the humidifier in the immediate area, I don't have spider mites. Then all I have to do is look for the other pests, which are not so disastrous or so invasive to a plant collection. By the way, you won't be able to see spider mites unless you have good eyes. Their webbing in a plant's axils and under leaves is the only indication. But be assured of one thing: You will have pests if you don't use preventive measures.

As winter arrives and most of us make only the necessary trips to work and the grocery store, we know that before long the arctic air masses will descend, one after another, and slam into our north windows. We'll try to stay close to home on cold, nasty days, and inside altogether on icy, snowy days. But civilization won't come to a halt—we can always carry on business by fax, phone, and e-mail. Technology is great. But it's the sight of something green growing in a pot that really gets us through the winter.

Keep your pots clean

In the spring, some houseplant gardeners set their plants on bricks or blocks of wood instead of directly on the patio. They say it keeps pots a bit cleaner. But John, a fellow gardener, prefers to keep his plants higher up on tables and benches. He also found specially made wrought-iron plant stands for his collection of smaller pots. As a result, he has almost no messy pots to clean in the fall.

Rosemary

I like to keep prostrate rosemary over the winter each year. I grow it in large urns, where in the summer it receives the warmth, air circulation, and bright light it loves so much. During the winter months I bring it in, where it makes a soft, gray-green, aromatic carpet in its travels across the stone floor. If I left it outside, it would die during our crazy up-and-down Tennessee winters, and I'd have to start all over again trying to grow it long and flowing. You fortunate people who live where the weather is always warm and not so finicky can keep rosemary outside year-round. Grow it on your stone wall and let it drape where it will, softening as it crawls about.

CHAPTER TWELVE VACATIONING AND MOVING

For those people who find summer travel hot, sweaty, and inconvenient (I include myself among these people), vacations are reserved for late fall and winter. These months are trouble-free. Temperatures are cool, trees are changing into their fall colors, and the smell of burning leaves replaces flower fragrances. Vacations are enjoyed, and everything in the plant room is either resting or dormant. Water needs are unimportant, and demands upon plant tenders are minimal.

But people who vacation during the spring and summer leave when houseplants make their greatest demands on their owners. Spring and summer are the seasons when water needs increase sharply for plants because they're adding new growth, expanding their roots, replicating themselves as offsets, and producing flowers. Many potted plants use up their supply of water so fast that they need it daily, especially if they're summering outdoors, and most basket plants need watering twice a day.

So how do you water everything outside or in the plant room when you're away from one to three weeks during the summer? You have several options.

Use Plant Sitters

Friends are the first who come to mind as plant sitters. They know you, and they know your routine of caring for your plants. They're probably plant people themselves and realize certain plant culture no-no's such as no evening watering. If you've sheltered your plants outside, friends can drop in for a quick check to make sure everything's battened down when those unexpected, late-afternoon thunderstorms produce their half-hour sound-and-light shows before moving on. Your friends will tend your plants as you would tend them.

Asking garden friends to look in each day is your best option. Here's why:
- They won't be miffed if you leave a list of special care instructions for plants they may not be familiar with.
- They know your house.
- They know your plants.
- They know your garden room, including its advantages and disadvantages.
- They live close to you and can keep an eye on other things as well: mail, packages, unexpected visitors, power outages, air-conditioner problems, emergency calls from family, and grass that's growing too fast.
- They're trusted.
- They're experienced in caring for plants.
- They know how to detect insect problems and can alert you to them on your return.
- They also can feed, care, and provide company for lonesome pets.
- They can make the house look lived in until you return.
- They can pass along important answering-machine messages to you.

If you intend to be gone for several weeks, you may feel better about paying a friend to plant-sit. It's worth it. It'll also save your pet the dreaded stay at the vet's office.

If your friend refuses payment, make his or her plant-sitting tasks as enjoyable as possible. Here are a few suggestions.

- Stock the fridge with your friend's favorite food.
- Leave the latest videos on top of the VCR.
- Put several discount coupons on the counter for late-night pizza and have some cold drinks waiting.
- Leave the latest gardening books and magazines on the sofa in plain view.
- Invite your friend to stay for several days as your guest in your home.

This last prospect is one I find charming. It's a variation on the old English idea of "letting" one's home for the summer.

During the last century when some well-to-do English and European families went on their vacations (referred to as "holidays"), they "let" their homes for two or three months during the summer. This meant that they took in paying guests to live in their home while they went off to enjoy their own holiday. This was an ingenious idea: Go off on vacation and have someone live in your house and pay you for doing it.

The prospect of staying as a guest (nonpaying, of course) in a friend's home while looking after plants and premises is appealing to me. If a friend lived far away, I, too, could go on a little holiday even though I was rendering a service to a friend. You may want to consider this idea, especially if your friend lives out of state. A little trip might be enjoyable for you both.

Rotate your friends as plant sitters

While our friends would be willing to do anything for us, they also have their own obligations (and plants) to care for during the summer months. But I believe that people don't find this type of thing quite so bothersome if they know it won't last long. So you might try this: Ask several friends to plant-sit, each for only three days on a rotating basis. After Sue puts in her three days, Frank takes over for his, then John, and so on. Later, favors can be repaid similarly.

I find that this works well for extended holidays and trips abroad. If you plan to be gone for a month, ask each friend to plant-sit for one week. Assuming that you can round up four friends, your problem is solved. Having a friend plant-sit for you is better than being beset by constant worries that something will be left undone.

Employ a "real" plant sitter

There *are* agencies that hire out plant sitters. In addition, some people advertise in the local newspapers as house or plant sitters. If an agency appeals to you, be sure to ask what services they offer and if a contract is needed. For your own protection, a contract of some kind would be advisable. It's also good business to ask for a printed list of services and rates. If the agency has people available who know plant care, these are the sitters to ask for.

And it may ease your mind a bit if you ask to speak to the sitters to determine just how much expertise they do have, especially if you'll be gone for a long period. And just to be on the safe side, it never hurts to provide your own list of duties, explaining clearly what you wish done for your plants and when. One final thought: It's always a good idea to check the references of anyone you intend to hire. It's better to be safe than sorry.

Ask a retired relative to plant-sit

Retired relatives make wonderful plant sitters. Mature family members understand you and your needs and are eager to please. Invite an adventuresome couple into your home as your guests. If they're from out of town, provide them with road maps and a list of things to see while they visit. It may prove to be just the brief, inexpensive vacation they're looking for.

Provide a list of duties, explaining clearly what you wish done for your plants and when, and leave their favorite food, drinks, videos, and magazines in the house. Also consider treating them to dinner or making a salon appointment for them. Provide them with a list of phone numbers in case electrical emergencies or other problems should arise. They will feel obligated to protect your property as if it were their own.

Prepare Your Plants to Fend for Themselves

Preparing your plants to fend for themselves is not as cavalier as it sounds. You can leave your plants unattended for long periods if you make a few adjustments in the way you water them. The methods I discuss here apply only to plants that stay *indoors* during the summer. Those outdoors under the rose arbor must be cared for by a person, simply because they require more water more often.

The first thing you need to do is determine how often you usually water your indoor plants under normal air-conditioner settings. *Normal* means what temperature you usually set your air-

conditioner on in the summer. I suggest that for the duration of your vacation, however, you lower the setting. If you're used to a 78°F indoor temperature, it would be wise to lower the temp in the house to 75°F for the comfort of the plants and because the plants will use less water.

Once you determine how often you would water your plants during the time you'll be gone, you need to choose strategies that'll help deliver the water at the rate you estimate your plants will need it. Then I recommend that you test the system. In other words, use the methods of watering you decide on for about a week before you plan to leave. This allows you the opportunity to see that they actually function according to your needs. You'll also have enough time to make any last-minute changes.

Here are some suggestions for helping your plants make it on their own.

Self-watering containers

Many people use self-watering containers throughout the year for all their small plants. If you plan to use these devices on a permanent basis, you need to monitor soil moisture occasionally to make sure the plants don't receive too much or too little water. You'll also need to check the wick now and then to make sure it's functioning properly.

To make your own self-watering container for temporary vacation care, begin collecting butter, margarine, or other plastic containers with lids; you'll need one container with lid for each plant. Your friends also can help by saving containers for you. I prefer clear plastic containers because they allow me to view the water level. If it gets low, I know at a glance that I need to add water to the container.

But don't use just any plastic container. Make sure the container can be filled with at least 2 cups of water. The small margarine tubs hold only a little over a cup, so you'll want larger sizes. Also check to see that the plastic lid is able to support the weight of a small pot when it's snapped into place on top of the container—remember that clay pots are heavy.

Once you have all of your containers and lids, wash everything in hot, soapy water, and begin making your self-watering devices. Here's what you do:

1. Water each potted plant.

2. Make two holes in each plastic lid. One hole should be near the center of the lid—exact measurements aren't necessary. This hole must be big enough for the wick to pass through. Make a second hole off to the side, to be used for adding water. (After skewering myself once with an ice pick, I learned to stack three lids together at a time and use a drill to make all the holes at once.)

Self-watering pots allow your plants to fend for themselves when you're on vacation.

Making a self-watering pot

1. Carefully remove the plant from its pot.

2. Make a hole in the plastic lid for the wick.

3. Thread a cotton or nylon wick through one of the pot's drainage holes.

4. Using a stick or pencil, pass the wick into the root ball, then repot the plant.

5. Fill the container with water, replace the lid, and set the pot on top, making sure the wick is in the water.

3. Fashion a wick for each plant. Use an 8-in.-long piece of cotton or nylon material for the wick. I like to use cotton cloth cut into strips about $\frac{1}{2}$ in. wide, but old nylon pantyhose work well, too. You may prefer more or less than 8 in. for your wicks.

4. Unpot the plant. Working with one plant at a time, take it out of its pot, keeping the root ball intact.

5. Pass the wick into the pot. Push the wick through one of the drainage holes in the bottom of the pot. Leave some of the wick dangling from the bottom of the pot.

6. Pass the wick up into the plant. Use a pencil or a small stick to push the end of the wick up into the root ball.

7. Repot the plant. Make sure that a length of wick hangs out the drainage hole of the pot.

8. Put it all together. Fill the plastic container with water. Push the wick through the center hole in the lid and put the lid on the container. Now set the pot on the lid. The wick should be well down in the water, and the plant should be sitting in a stable position on the lid.

It's a good idea to keep plants and their wicking containers out of direct sun, or else your plants will use up their water supply too quickly.

Wick watering works for plants in plastic and clay pots; however, the clay pots will use up water at a faster rate because clay is porous. You may want to use a deeper plastic container for your clay pots to ensure that these are adequately supplied with all the water they need. If you find that you like this method of watering and want to use it again in the future, save all of your containers and lids. Put them into a large heavy-duty plastic bag or cardboard box

and store them in the attic or basement. The next time you need them, they'll be ready for use. Cut new wicks each time you use the containers, however, so that you don't transfer problems from the soil of one pot to the soil of another.

Shared reservoir watering

Shared reservoir watering allows you to group large and small plants together for a communal watering. One centralized container of water is used, but you'll give each plant its own wick. All of them can then drink from the same source. This method is for those gardeners who hate to collect butter containers and don't have time to drill holes. Because the plants will not have their own reservoirs, you must use a container large enough to hold sufficient water for all the plants.

Here's the way to make a shared reservoir system.

1. Water each pot.

2. Fashion a wick for each plant. Use a long piece of cotton or nylon material for the wicks. Cotton cloth torn into strips or old nylon pantyhose work fine. You'll have to estimate the length. Begin with long pieces and cut them down.

3. Pass the wick down into each plant from the soil surface. Use a pencil to push the end of the wick down through the soil. Bury the wick deeply.

4. Put it all together. Fill a deep pan or bucket with water. Set it in the middle of your grouped plants, with the plants on a level lower than the water source. Place each plant's wick down into the water so that they all share the same water source. If the wicks float to the surface, put a stone on top of each to hold it down in the water.

Be sure to keep the reservoir out of the sun, so the water won't evaporate before the plants can use it. When you come back from your vacation, simply dispose of the wicks and pour the water out—there's nothing to store.

Capillary mats

Have you ever left the corner of a towel hanging into a sink of water? When you came back to it an hour later, most of the towel was wet, even though only a small part of it was in the water. This is the idea behind a capillary mat. Capillary mats are made of felt, which holds water. When part of the mat is placed in water, the other part—which lies on the drainer surface of your sink—also becomes wet because water is wicked up into it. Plants sitting on the mat absorb the water up through the bottom of their pots.

These mats are good if you have a small number of plants and can group them on the counter next to your sink. The idea works best for plants in plastic pots, but clay pots can be used if you make an adjustment. Clay pots would readily absorb the water for themselves (they're porous) and leave the plants' root balls dry, so it's important to add a wick to each clay pot you set on a capillary mat. The wick will bring the water up from the mat and into the pot so that the root ball remains moist.

Here's how to set up this system.
1. Water each pot.
2. Fill the sink partially with water.
3. Place two-thirds of the capillary mat on the counter.
4. Drop the other third of the mat into the water and flatten it out.
5. Group your pots together on top of the mat on the counter.

If your trip is to be a long one, make sure that your plants have a light source near them, but don't let them sit in direct sunlight—they'll use water at a faster rate. Also, allow the tap to drip slowly into the sink. A constant drip will be enough to replace any evaporating water, especially if the window is out of direct sunlight.

Bathtub wicking

I used the bathtub wicking method when I lived in an apartment and had very little space. I was new to houseplant gardening at the time and had simply reasoned out this method myself. Since those days, I've seen the idea in houseplant gardening books, so I was evidently on the right track. This system calls for newspaper to protect the surface of your tub and bricks to keep the pots up and out of standing water. I like this method because you can put a lot of plants in a bathtub, including large trees.

The method has only one drawback: When you remove the newspaper, you have newsprint on your tub. If you don't mind this, you easily can remove the black print by cleaning your tub as usual.

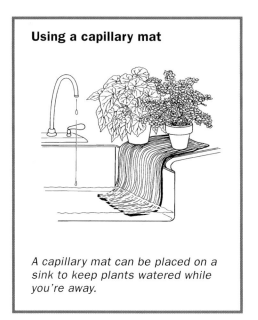

Using a capillary mat

A capillary mat can be placed on a sink to keep plants watered while you're away.

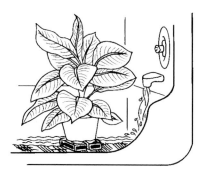

Setting up
a bathtub wicking system

Large plants can benefit from being in the bathtub. Place towels or newspaper on the bottom, elevate the plant on bricks, and fill the tub with water to cover the bricks.

But here's a material I like better than the newspaper: old towels. Yes, it means you'll have to wash them all when you return, but it's that or clean off newsprint and throw away lots of soggy newspapers. Which would you rather do?

Here's how to set up a bathtub wicking system to cover the bricks:

1. Water each pot.

2. Place overlapping sheets of newspaper or old towels on the bottom of your tub.

3. Set bricks on top of the newspaper.

4. Place your plants on top of the bricks.

5. Cover the newspaper and bricks with water from the tap. Bring the water level up to the top of the bricks, barely covering them with water.

You can't use this method for much more than a week unless you have a well-lit bathroom—plants need light. When I did this 30 years ago, there was no window in the bathroom. The plants didn't have light for a week, but this

didn't bother them. In the summer, plants have enough stored energy to last them that long, but keeping them in a bathroom more than a week without a light is inadvisable.

Here's another trick you might like. It'll add humidity around your plants and discourage spider mites, the bane of indoor plants. After filling the tub to the proper level, pull the shower curtain closed, keeping it to the outside of the tub. Your plants will stay humid as well as watered.

Plastic bags

The plastic bag method is simple and doesn't call for standing water. But you will have to save clear dry-cleaning bags. Here's how to protect your small- and medium-sized plants with bags:

1. Water each pot.

2. Sink thin, tall sticks into the soil around the perimeter of the pot—three or four usually suffice. The sticks keep

Enclosing a plant in a plastic bag

Loosely covering plants with a plastic bag helps them maintain moisture. Sticks keep the plastic away from the plant.

the plastic up and away from the foliage. Rot is likely to occur if plant foliage comes in contact with the plastic.

3. Cover your plant with a plastic bag.

4. Secure the bag to the rim of the pot—I use rubber bands on small pots.

I don't like this method for long-term use, even though it's recommended by some houseplant books as a strategy for keeping pots moist for two to three weeks. I used it once when I was away for over a week and wasn't pleased with the results when I removed the bags. The plants do stay moist, and that's the problem. I've already talked about air circulation and its importance to plants. So when I tell you that I battled rot and fungus for weeks after I returned home, you'll understand.

Covering a plant with plastic and then closing it off holds in moisture, but it also prevents air circulation around your plant's foliage. Still conditions allow for a constantly warm, moist environment— just the right ingredients for fungus and rot to begin.

But here's another option for long-term trips: Instead of securing the bag with a rubber band, leave the bag open. Simply drape the plastic bag over the sticks, and let it hang loosely from there. At least a little air will be able to enter the bag and flow around.

If you decide to try the closed-bag method for periods of no more than a week, you may be pleased at how well this system works.

A word of caution: Don't put your plastic-covered plants in the window so that full sun can heat them up. You know what the sun does to anything that's in a plastic bag—the high temperatures will cook your plants.

Wet packing method #1

If you have small pots, wet packing works well. Medium pots will require large, deep containers. Wet packing is a good method to use, because air will be able to circulate around your plants, and their pots will continue to stay moist for a week.

You'll need one or more large pans, depending on how many pots you can fit into each pan. I like those deep, disposable (and cheap) turkey-roasting pans (you can find them in grocery stores). I always buy a couple of packages whenever I see them. When I get the pans home, I put them in a heavy plastic bag and take them to the attic, where they stay until I need them.

In addition to your pan(s), you'll also need material that can serve as packing: old newspapers, peat moss, or long-fiber sphagnum moss. Old newspaper is cheapest. But if you use a lot of peat moss or long-fiber sphagnum moss for double-potting, you may want to use it instead of newspaper.

Wet packing provides plants with humidity and a water supply.

Here's how to wet pack your plants:

1. Water each pot.
2. Put your pots in the pan(s).
3. Wet the packing material and stuff it between the pots. Don't wring the water out of the packing material very much before you put it into the pan. You want the packing to stay moist over a period of time. This also means, of course, that the plants in the packing material should be kept out of the sun so that drying doesn't occur.

Wet packing method #2

This wet packing strategy works well for long vacations (if plants are kept out of the sun). Follow wet packing method #1, with one addition: Connect a small hose to the faucet and allow it to drip very slowly into the pan. I found a small hose in a catalog from a hobby greenhouse company. It screws onto the kitchen tap and is made for watering indoor plants. Hobby greenhouse clubs in your area probably can tell you where to buy one locally. With this method, the water will be wicked through the packing, which will stay moist (not wet) for a longer time.

It's important, however, that you test this method before leaving it to run on its own. Experiment with it for a few days to see that the packing stays evenly moist and that the dripping hose adds only tiny amounts of water. Since you may be leaving for a long trip, you will need to place the pans near a light source. Avoid strong light, because the packing could dry out more quickly than the dripping water can moisten it.

Other Things to Consider

Your growing conditions are different from mine. Take into consideration your own special conditions and make a decision about your watering method based upon them. You may even want to use a combination of different methods if your collection is a large one. Reviewing these facts will help you make the wisest choices. Plants need more water when they have been fertilized, are in hanging pots, are potted in clay pots, are underpotted, are actively growing, are flowering or putting on buds, or have large, thin leaves (like many tropicals). They'll also need more water when the temperature is high or when the humidity is low.

After you decide on a method or a combination of methods, you should do the following:

- Check the method you're using to see that it functions well *before* you leave.
- Keep plants out of strong light.
- Remove all buds and flower stalks, since flowers require more water.
- Turn the thermostat down so that plants will stay cool. This way, they'll use less water and stay moist longer.

Reviving a severely wilted plant

1. Scratch the soil surface.

2. Immerse the pot and mist the foliage.

What to Do if a Pot Completely Dries Out

There's always one in the bunch that'll completely dry out. If you return home to find a plant wilted and bone dry, all may not be lost. There's a chance that it can be revived. If cellular collapse is caught in time, it can be reversed in most cases—but not all.

Take these steps as soon as possible:

1. Loosen the soil. Take the pot to the sink and loosen the soil with a fork, working all around the pot. Be careful not to damage the roots.

2. Submerge the pot in water. Fill the sink with warm water up to the rim of the pot. Mist the foliage and let the plant sit in the water for a half-hour (you'll have to hold the pot in place for a while until it takes on water; it'll want to float).

3. Check the plant after a half-hour to see if it has revived. Mist the leaves again and return the plant to its place.

Plants for Travelers

If you are gone several months out of the year and using a capillary mat just isn't for you, you can grow plants that don't require close attention to watering. The following low-water plants are beautiful when in bloom, and some of them remain in bloom for months at a time: bromeliads, cacti, and some succulents.

But if you want something completely different, try keeping plants in a closed environment—a terrarium or bottle garden. These are protected environments that don't require constant attention.

What to Do if You Have to Move

More people are packing up their tents and moving to greener pastures these days. Families are much more mobile.

They have to be ready to pull up stakes and move at the drop of a hat.

We take our environment (our paintings, books, furniture, and CD collection) with us wherever we go—our environment is an extension of our personalities. And for some of us, plants are very much a part of that environment. They travel with us. The difference is that they're living things, not inanimate objects like a couch or a stereo, and they may have something to say about the way they've been treated a few weeks after reaching their destination. Plants have been known to take travel poorly, and this doesn't surprise me because they do so much of it. They travel from the greenhouse or the nursery where they were first "born" and first potted up, to the garden center where they sit and wait to be claimed, to their first home with you, and then on to any later homes you move into.

Houseplants are seldom exposed to the excellent growing conditions of their native environment. And although they do adapt in some measure to the varied conditions they find themselves in, they can't adapt as an animal would by simply running away if the situation is too much to put up with. If it gets to that point, the plant simply gives up and dies because it's used up the extent of its resources for staying alive. A potted plant can adapt just so much.

How to move your plants

If your move is a short one, your plants can be taken to their new home independent of the household furniture. Longer trips will require more planning. Your plants should be the last things packed and the first things unpacked.

If you are moving, use newspaper wrapping to protect your small and medium plants from damaged leaves and broken stems.

Take stock of how many plants you have

How many plants of one kind do you have? For example, how many cacti do you have? Keep small plants like this together. If there are plants that you know won't make the trip well, or if the weather is extremely cold, give them to gardening friends, have a plant sale, or present them to a surprised, but grateful beginner. After all, you can always buy new plants when you get to where you're going.

The day before you begin packing Water each pot the day before you begin packing up. The only exception is cacti—let them travel dry. Plants will have had one day to drink and dry before going, and your car and trunk won't be troubled by water damage. Keep an old absorbent throw in the trunk so that wet pots won't cause any damage. If your throw is big enough, it can be snuggled up against the pots to steady them.

Packing up your plants

• **Small pots.** Wrap each pot in newspaper, and set the plants into cardboard boxes. Or simply set the pots into the boxes, and stuff crumpled newspaper between the pots to keep them from moving about.

• **Medium plants.** These can be wrapped in newspaper. Lay the plant on its side and begin rolling it up in newspaper. If possible, encase the foliage. Use rubber bands to hold the newspaper in place, or stack the wrapped plants side by side in big boxes without using rubber bands. Medium plants also can be covered with plastic bags from the dry cleaners; secure them with rubber bands. This way, you can keep them in a humid mini-environment—this might alleviate leaf-drop later on.

• **Tall plants.** I rented a small moving van to transport my plants from one state to another during the summer. They rode well despite the more than 90°F heat. Don't use a professional moving company to move your plants along with your furniture. They often "gang" several shipments together, and probably won't guarantee the condition of your plants. If renting a small moving van is out of the question, the trunk of your car may be the only way. Tall plants will have to be laid down. A throw should be placed over the exposed portion of foliage to protect it from wind and heat, and the throw will have to be tied on so that it won't blow off. Don't use plastic, because it will heat up too much. A few bricks propped up against the container will keep it from rolling about. And, finally, you must keep the trunk of the car from bouncing up and down on the plant if it's hanging out the back of the car. You can double-wrap the plant's trunk in thick towels as added protection, but the car's trunk also must be tied with stout cord or clothesline.

- **Heavy plants.** Determine how you'll deal with the weight of heavy plants. I recommend a two-wheel dolly, a child's wagon, or a plant dolly. Plant dollies look like platforms on wheels. They're usually made of wood and have wheels (or casters) under them so they can be pushed along. You'll find them at garden centers in different sizes, and they're inexpensive considering the alternative if you should wrench your back. Once the plant's in the general area, slide it onto a rug and drag it where you want it. This will save your back and your energy. Tilt the plant, remove the rug, and insert a large drip saucer underneath.

While traveling Don't leave plants in a hot car during the summer. They can collapse from the heat and die within minutes. The temperature in a closed car on a hot day can reach more than 120°F. Plants, pets, and children have no business in a closed car in the heat of the summer without air-conditioning. Consider eating your meals in the car so that all the windows can be rolled down or the air-conditioner can be turned on.

When you arrive When you get where you're going, put your plants in similar light exposures to the ones they just left. Provide extra humidity and don't feed them for a few months. Mist your plants soon after reaching your destination.

Be prepared for the plants to react to their new surroundings: They may drop leaves. Plants, pets, and children hate to move as much as you do, but it doesn't have to be a distasteful process. Each must acclimate to the new surroundings,

and this will take time. Sometimes all three settle in well. But most of the time your pets will refuse food, become incontinent, want to stay close to you for reassurance, and every now and again, venture around the home on exploring expeditions. Ditto for the kids. But your plants will voice their difficulty by turning yellow and dropping leaves or refusing to put on new foliage for weeks. It'll take all three several weeks or months to settle in.

It's not unusual for plants to take a year to acclimate to new surroundings. I remember having difficulty with two plants on two separate occasions: One plant was a mature *Clivia miniata* with an offset; the other was a beautiful glory-bower *(Clerodendrum thomsoniae).* Both plants took one full year to adjust. There's nothing you can do but check the plant's cultural requirements and make sure you're following them. The rest is up to the plant.

TIPS

Frequent traveling
If you travel constantly or have such a busy daily schedule that time can't be spared for watering plants individually, you may want to switch all of your plants to self-watering pots.

Some of you may have busy times of the year. For example, if you are less busy in the winter, you may prefer to tend to your plants personally during the slack time but convert to self-watering containers during the hectic summer months.

This chapter is for beginners, certainly, but it's also for those gardeners who've been growing houseplants all along—and just want something a little different. They're tired of the usual spathiphyllums, dracaenas, and dieffenbachias. There are some good plants for indoor container culture, and some of them will be familiar to you, although you may not have thought of them as container plants.

Unusual Bloomers

Beginners may even want to try these if they think they need something easy but different. I either grow or have grown all of the plants discussed here indoors and can attest to their easy culture. As with everything, however, one must get the feel of new plants, and to this end, I've tried to give you cultural notes from a more personal perspective in the hope that your success with each of them may be ensured.

Amaryllis (Hippeastrum species)

Description Amaryllis bulbs are not a waste of money. They can be reflowered again the next year without difficulty, and you can enjoy the flowers for years to come. There's never any reason to throw away an amaryllis. You've seen these bulbs for sale during the Christmas season. Displays at garden centers and grocery stores feature four or more colors and offer individually boxed bulbs complete with pot, mix, and blooming-size bulb.

Bulb size is *everything* to an amaryllis grower—the bigger the bulb, the larger and more plentiful the blooms. A large bulb is also more expensive. But if you keep your bulbs growing properly from year to year, you can have a bulb worth four times what you paid for it. As the bulbs enlarge, they'll also make replicas

Amaryllis bulbs will give you years of large, plentiful blooms. (Photo by Alan Detrick.)

of themselves in the form of offsets, which you can nurture along into full-size bulbs within a few years. Consider the initial outlay of money as a long-term investment.

Amaryllises are identified by color or by cultivar name. They're sometimes identified simply as red, pink, orange, or white. But the superior bulbs are sold by cultivar, such as 'Red Lion', 'Apple Blossom', and 'Scarlet Admiral'.

When you pot them up and they finish blooming a month later, you should keep them growing as you would any houseplant. It's important that the bulb gain nourishment and strength to send up another two flower stalks the next year, and it can't do this if you cut off or neglect the foliage.

Culture

- **Light.** When in flower, give amaryllises as much sun as possible. This creates a smaller, stockier stalk—they'll look as if they had been grown in the greenhouse. They're also less likely to become top heavy and tip over.

  When amaryllis summer outside, give them full sun. Their pots can be plunged, or the bulbs can be planted directly into the soil—they look good planted en masse in the perennial border. Some plant directories tell you to put them in bright light with no direct sun. But I've found that they don't flower well when it comes time for them to bloom. They will need several hours of sun each day in the summer, if you can't keep them in full sun.

- **Water.** Newly planted bulbs that have just been purchased and potted up should be watered thoroughly only one time until you see greenery pushing up through the soil. If you give amaryllis bulbs too much water at this stage,

there's a chance of rot. Also, look at it this way: A newly potted bulb has no roots or leaves that will use the water you give it. All you succeed in doing is keeping the bulbs wet, and this rots them every time.

Even if I'm reflowering a bulb, I don't water again after the first warm drink until I see green. Even if the bulb has plenty of roots, it could *still* rot.

When in flower, keep your amaryllis moist, but not wet. Allow the soil to dry a little between waterings, and then soak it thoroughly until you see water pour from the drainage hole. After flowering, continue to water—the plant is still in its growth cycle.

- **Temperature.** When potting up a newly purchased bulb, keep it in a warm room to get the flower stalk up. The warmer the room, the quicker the stalk appears. Then move it to a cooler room when the flowers begin to open. Cool temps will keep the plant in bloom longer. After the amaryllis flowers, move it back into the warmth with your other tropicals.
- **Humidity.** Same as tropicals: 50%.
- **Potting.** Use a light potting soil, and keep the bulbs in the same pot as long as possible—they like tight places and bloom better if under these conditions. If the pot's too large, you'll have great-looking leaves—but no flowers. I keep a bulb in its pot for three or four years, then repot it into a slightly larger pot.

  I put my bulbs into clay pots that are only 1 in. larger than the bulbs. Some people prefer a slightly larger pot—one that's 2 in. larger. I like to use clay pots for amaryllises because there's less chance of overwatering, the weight will keep a top-heavy plant from tipping over, and they look better in clay pots than in plastic pots.

Another safety precaution against rot is to let half the bulb show above the soil when you plant it. The roots will hold the plant in the pot because they'll fill the space quickly.

- **Feeding.** Feed with an all-purpose food (20-20-20) after the plant stops blooming and into the summer.

Tips For a truly beautiful container of blooms in succession, plant several bulbs (three or five) of the *same* color or cultivar in a clay pot. Groupings are much prettier than single plantings.

Here's how to reflower your amaryllis after it blooms the first time:

- Cut off the blooms and flower stalk.
- Move the plant to a sunny window.
- Let the foliage continue to grow during winter.
- Water as usual.
- Fertilize with water-soluble plant food.

In the summer, take the bulb outdoors when night temps are *consistently* above 55°F. Plant the bulb in full sun in the garden so that it gets at least four hours of sun a day. The soil should be loose and well drained. We have clay soils in Tennessee, so I always dig a large hole, back fill it with good, loose potting soil, and plant my bulb in it. You also can plunge the entire pot or set it on the patio in the sun. During dry periods, water it as you would your other plants. And fertilize as you do your other houseplants.

During the first week in September, dig up the bulb or pot if you had planted it in the garden. Cut the foliage back so it is 1 in. above the bulb. Repot the bulb if it spent the summer in your garden soil. When repotting:

- Use a porous, well-drained potting soil in a clay pot that's 1 in. larger than the bulb.

Delicate fanflowers trail beautifully out of a pot.

- Leave half of the bulb showing above the soil.
- If you'd like, add ⅓ in. of coarse builder's sand on top of the soil to weight the pot and promote drainage.

Don't water or fertilize the bulb at this point. Put the pot in the garage, an unheated room in the house, or other cool place that won't get below 40°F—do not let the bulb freeze. Keep the pot elevated (on a table or shelf up off the floor) where it's a bit warmer. It's not necessary to give the bulb any light at this time—it's resting.

Here's how to bring the bulb back into bloom:

- During the last week in November, bring the pot inside the house or other heated area.
- Clean up the pot and water the bulb thoroughly with *warm water.*
- Set the pot in a warm place, and don't water again until you see green growth emerging from the soil.
- When the stalk grows to 6 in., begin to water the plant.

After the plant finishes flowering, it's time to start the yearly cycle again.

Fanflower (Scaevola aemula)

Description I have nothing but praise for fanflower, a basket plant. The 'New Wonder' variety is now on the market and worth every penny. If you like a basket plant you can grow in full sun and leave outdoors to flower all summer, this is the one for you. It's carefree and so vigorous that I plant it into the perennial border in the spring and watch it mingle with other plants as it spreads.

The flowers are blue or pink and fan shaped, with bright yellow centers; the foliage is attractive and neat. The plant is a sun lover and takes our Tennessee heat like a real trouper. It's a quick spreader and a low grower (6 in. to 8 in. tall) in the perennial border, too. And as a hanging basket plant, it'll grow a surprising 2 ft. in six weeks. You can grow it in tubs, urns (I grow it in urns with prostrate rosemary), and window boxes. It's not often you see such versatility in a plant.

Culture

- **Light.** Place fanflower in your sunniest exposure indoors or in full sun outdoors. More sun means more flowers. If you can't manage full sun, position fanflower in the brightest light you have.
- **Water.** Keep it watered if you plant it in a container, but if you plant it in your outdoor beds, water sparingly.
- **Temperature.** Fanflower should be brought in with your other plants in the fall because it can't tolerate temps lower than 28°F.
- **Humidity.** Same as tropicals: 50%.
- **Potting.** Use a well-drained potting soil. Since this plant likes humus, you can mix in a handful of finely chopped leaves when you repot it.
- **Feeding.** Feed the same way you feed your other plants, or use African violet food.

Tip When I grow hanging basket plants, I usually pinch the plants back so that I get more stems and, therefore, more flowers. But pinching doesn't appear necessary to keep stems and flowers coming on fanflower. The 'New Wonder' variety is a plant that belongs in the sunniest window of your plant room.

Jasmine (Jasminum *species*)

Description I see large numbers of jasmines offered for sale each year. I used to spot them in grocery stores during the winter months, but now garden centers carry them throughout the year. You'll enjoy growing any of the jasmine species, and your plant room or greenhouse will stay constantly perfumed with sweet fragrance—you won't want to leave it.

I particularly like jasmine during the winter when everything's under a thick blanket of snow outside. This is the time when jasmine usually blooms. Any of these plants grow well indoors, and you'll have a steady supply of blooms as long as they get the bright light and humidity they need. You can grow them as trailers in hanging baskets or as shrubs if you keep them pinched back. By spring, they'll probably be ready to be repotted, because they grow quickly in the winter.

Culture

- **Light.** Jasmine is a plant to summer outside in an unsheltered area—it likes four to six hours of sun. If you can only manage four hours of sun and the rest of the day in bright light, the plant won't complain. Indoors, keep it in a sunny south- or west-facing window, and it'll bloom its head off.
- **Water.** Don't let the soil dry out— keep it moist.
- **Temperature.** Most species like 60° to 80°F. But if you prefer to keep your greenhouse or plant room cool in the winter and can't heat it to 60°F, try *J. polyanthum.* This sturdy vine is a winter jasmine that can take 45° to 55°F easily; it bears blooms from February into the spring.
- **Humidity.** Give jasmine high humidity: 55% at least. Keep your warm steam humidifier near the plant in the winter. If you summer the plant outdoors, puddle the area around it

Clouds of jasmine flowers emit a wonderful fragrance. (Photo by Erik Simmons.)

with standing water so that it'll be bathed in moist air.

- **Potting.** Use a rich, humusy potting soil. I've added finely chopped leaves to the potting mix, and the plant seems to like it.
- **Feeding.** I've found that jasmines flower more and longer if they're fed with African violet food. They usually rest for a few weeks after a heavy flush of growth, but can be brought back into bloom by using a food high in phosphorus, such as African violet fertilizer. During the summer, give the plant fish emulsion for one of your monthly feedings.

Tip When you rake leaves in the fall, chop up a large mound with your lawn mower, and put the leaves in a large plastic trash can. Then add some of the leaves to your potting mix when you repot your jasmine in the spring.

Lily of the Nile or agapanthus (Agapanthus africanus)

Description If you like growing amaryllises, you'll like lily of the Nile. The foliage looks like an amaryllis, but, of course, this is a different plant. And in some ways, I think this plant is prettier, with its larger straplike leaves and its impressive head of blue, tubular flowers atop tall stalks. It blooms in the summer and is easy to care for. But you'll need room for it; it's a large plant (there are also smaller varieties you can choose from). Agapanthus makes an excellent accent plant for a sunny corner of your plant room or greenhouse; and when it's finished blooming, it's a handsome foliage plant.

Summer the plant outdoors, but bring it back in with your other plants in the fall, because it must have a frost-free environment.

Lily of the Nile's large flowers make this plant a great addition to your collection. (Photo by Paddy Wales.)

Culture

- **Light.** Put lily of the Nile in the sunniest spot possible or in bright light.
- **Water.** It needs more water when in flower. Keep the soil moist in the summer, and cut back on watering from November to April.
- **Temperature.** Bring indoors before the first frost. Grow at the same temperature as your other plants.
- **Humidity.** Same as tropicals: 50%.
- **Potting.** Use well-drained potting soil and grow lily of the Nile in tubs or large pots. But don't repot until the container is full of overcrowded plants—it will bloom better this way.
- **Feeding.** Feed with African violet food starting in the spring when growth begins.

Night-blooming cereus (Epiphyllum oxypetalum)

Description You may not be able to find night-blooming cereus easily, but it's worth trying to locate. Almost everyone who has it was given a small piece to root and, from that piece, has been able to grow this spectacular jungle plant. It's not like anything you've ever grown before, and there isn't much literature on it. Plant directories often don't mention it.

The foliage is unusual but not overly impressive. In fact, it looks very much like a large orchid. The leaves are elongated and set along a whiplike stem that rises up out of the center of the plant. From the large, thick, leathery-looking leaves come the most exquisite flowers I've ever seen. Nothing compares to their beauty or size. Orchid growers may not agree with me, but I don't think any orchid can hold a candle to a cereus bloom.

Night-blooming cereus

The opening of a flower bud is a big production at my house. The bud will open only at night and for only *one* night. In the plant's native environment, the blooms are pollinated by bats and night-flying moths. The plant has very little time to make sure it gets pollinated, so it has to act fast. The bloom has three things that help it:

- It is white (or champagne)—easy to see on full-moon nights.
- It is *huge*, and hangs from a thick stem that's almost a foot long.
- It is fragrant—and more so when it's fully open.

I was surprised recently when buds began opening at 5:30 in the afternoon! We'd had sunless days for weeks and the blooms took advantage of it to open in daylight. This was a treat—I didn't have to walk around, flashlight in hand, until later that night to watch the bloom's complete unfurling. If you turn the lights on, you can see the flower begin to close, so flashlights are a must.

You'll know what night the bud will open because it'll swell by 3:00 P.M. The actual opening, however, doesn't start until about 9:00 P.M.—the perfect time for a late champagne supper. Each successive hour, the blossom unfolds until it's fully open by midnight. By 8:00 A.M., it's shriveled.

If you know someone who has this plant, ask for one old leaf—the older the better (or take anything you can get). A night-blooming cereus won't bloom on young foliage, so by asking for an old leaf, you'll get blooms sooner. Set the leaf somewhere out of the way for at least a week. This is called "callusing." The stem end of the leaf will harden and form a callous so that when you put it in soil, it won't rot. Do this when you're rooting succulents, and they'll take much better. To root the leaf:

1. Choose a small clay pot and crock it.
2. Add a light potting soil mix and warm water.
3. Put the limp leaf in the soil so that it stands up on its own.
4. Set the leaf in bright light with no direct sun.
5. Keep the soil barely moist. Soon, the leaf will take on water and become firm again.

Your leaf may not do anything for a few weeks because it must begin root growth first, but it'll send up a stalk and other leaves within a few months after it's planted. Leaves always take faster in the spring and summer, so if you try this in the fall or winter, the process is much slower.

Night-blooming cereus must be a monster in its own territory, because it's going to get large. You can allow it to reach a manageable height and then top it if you like, or if you keep it in the greenhouse, you can let it travel along the walls; you can anchor it to keep it parallel to the walls. The blooms will hang down if this is done. I've let mine grow to the top of the 13-ft. ceiling in my garden room.

I don't summer this plant outdoors at all. It's too big to move, and I want it under my eye at all times. But you certainly may put your plant in a bright sheltered area for the summer—just keep it out of the sun and remember to water it. It drinks like a fish during the summer once its roots begin growing.

Culture

- **Light.** Night-blooming cereus likes bright light, not full sun.
- **Water.** Keep the soil evenly moist in summer but drier in winter. Feel the soil first to see if the plant needs water. As with any plant you work with, it takes time to get the feel of a plant's culture. This one is no different.
- **Temperature.** My plant stays indoors at all times, and the temperature never gets above 76°F in the plant room; it dips into the 60s at night. If you summer your plant outdoors, puddle the patio area to bring up the humidity—remember that plants can take high heat as long as they also get high humidity.
- **Humidity.** Same as tropicals: 50%.
- **Potting.** Use a well-drained, porous potting mix.
- **Feeding.** I use African violet plant food.

Tip If you own *Epiphyllum oxypetalum,* as I do, and you're wondering how you can bring it into bloom more often, this might help. I discovered this trick by accident since the plant is seldom written up in houseplant books. Always keep

your ceiling fan on high in the plant room so that the night-blooming cereus has a constant breeze. If you have an air-conditioner in the same room, keep the room temperature at 74°F.

At night, the temperature will drop sufficiently (to the low 60s) for buds to set. More buds will set if the temp is driven down to between 50° and 60°F (it's a miracle they set at all during our hot, muggy Tennessee summers). Since I've used the ceiling fan and air-conditioner combination, I've had more blooms almost year-round—quite an accomplishment for a plant that doesn't bloom often in captivity.

Passionflower (Passiflora *species*)

Description Many years ago I lived in Mississippi for a brief period and was shocked to see blue passionflowers growing along the highway and in fields among the weeds. I tried to transplant them into pots, but they wouldn't have any of it, and I was never successful. I had no better luck with cuttings. And I got no help from books, either. At that time, the plant wasn't even in house-plant books, and you never saw it on the market—now it's everywhere and in more colors than my original blue.

This breathtaking vine (it can reach 20 ft.) sports peculiar fringed flowers. They'll bloom nonstop in the most attractive shades of blue, red, and purple if their cultural needs are met. Some of the cultivars are scented, but the wild ones I saw were not. Passionflower also produces a fruit, which can be eaten when ripe. If you want to grow the plant for this purpose, you'll need to try *P. edulis,* purple granadilla.

Passionflowers add that jungle touch to a plant room or greenhouse, especially if they're trained up and overhead. If you want to grow them in a small plant

The outrageous blooms of the passionflower plant add a jungly touch to your plant room. (Photo by Derek Fell.)

room, you can train them on a small wire cage and keep them clipped to a manageable height.

Culture

- **Light.** Because passionflowers must have at least four hours of sun and preferably six, the plants would love to summer out on the patio in plain view. A bright spot in the greenhouse also will satisfy them. Light is important to this plant. If it does not get the light it needs, the buds will wilt and drop.
- **Water.** The soil should be moist while the plant is in active growth. Reduce watering in the fall and winter when the plant's dormant, as you would your other plants.
- **Temperature.** This is a plant that likes to keep warm: 60°F or warmer suits it best in the winter.
- **Humidity.** Same as tropicals: 50%.
- **Potting.** A good, well-drained soil mix is fine. Grow passionflower in a large container and topdress each year with a few inches of new potting soil with compost added.
- **Feeding.** African violet food is fine.

Tip If you want fruit and your plants are indoors, you'll have to hand pollinate the flowers. A small artist's paintbrush is what you need. Take the pollen from the down-facing yellow anthers and transfer it to the ends of the stigmas, the structure in the center of each flower (it looks like a pinwheel to me). If your plants are summering outdoors, insects will pollinate them for you.

The Epiphytes

Bromeliads

Description The culture of bromeliads is the easiest of all plant cultures you're likely to encounter as you work with each family of plants. The bromeliads are not finicky plants. They are originally from the jungles, and they're epiphytes—air plants. Some grow in the crotches of trees and on branches in huge colonies (they aren't planted in soil), taking their nourishment and water from the rain, from bird and bat droppings, and from any other debris that happens to fall into their cups and on their leaves. Others are terrestrial, taking their nourishment from the loose soil in which they're planted. They require little, if any, soil about their roots.

Most bromeliads are beautiful when out of bloom and breathtaking when in bloom. And those blooms (or colored bracts), by the way, last from several weeks to months. After blooming, the plant slowly dies—it blooms only once. But before it dies (a process that may take as long as a few years), it makes offsets (referred to as "pups"), little replicas of itself to carry on in its place. And you don't get just one pup; you're likely to get several. What a way to increase your collection: Buy one expensive plant and you get several others free.

Culture As far as potting goes, in the sixties I used to be able to find osmunda fiber for repotting bromeliads and orchids, but I don't see osmunda anymore. Most people now use fir bark or mixes of peat and sphagnum for their bromeliads and orchids. Years ago, bromeliad growers used leaf mold, which they found in the woods, and mixed it with sharp sand, but this practice has probably fallen by the wayside.

I've found that bromeliads do better when watered with rainwater. Since I live in the country, I always have access to clean, fresh supplies of it. Those of you in the city may want to use tap water—one

Bromeliads come in stunning colors and don't require a lot of care. (Photo by Derek Fell.)

Propagating a bromeliad

Bromeliads sprout new plants called pups at the base of their stems. Propagate these by separating the pup from its parent, then potting it.

never knows what falls back to earth in the form of rain, and not just in industrialized areas.

Bromeliads aren't heavy feeders. Epiphytes have evolved to the point that they're experts at taking moisture and nutrients out of the air. So when you mix up your water-soluble fertilizer with warm water, pour some of it in a mister bottle and mist the leaves of all your bromeliads.

Why grow bromeliads? Bromeliads actually have *more* to offer the houseplant gardener than the usual tropical houseplant on the market: I think they're beautiful to look at (the colors are brilliant) even when they're not in spike. When they do bloom, they stay in flower for months.

They're easy to find, and they have begun to return to large grocery stores and garden centers. In the 1970s and early 1980s, you could find a huge assortment of bromeliads in food stores and chain department stores (before these stores had garden centers). Employees liked them because they required little or no care and weren't bothered by insects. I'm beginning to see their return to the grocery stores now. But you also can order them from catalogs (they can be sent through the mail without fear of damage), or visit your favorite family-owned garden center—they'll have them because they're becoming popular again.

Bromeliads aren't expensive, and they make so many pups that you get your money back and then some. They live for several years and make numerous offsets before they die. The offsets are easy to separate from the parent plant.

They aren't bothered by insect pests. You can kill them by overwatering, but paying attention to that cultural requirement isn't difficult. I once found a bromeliad in a trash heap and took it home to see what would happen if I potted it up. It pupped. All of the other cultural requirements are easy to meet, and you don't need any special equipment. Furthermore, bromeliads can be left unattended for weeks at a time. You don't have to constantly fetch and carry for them. They're tough and durable.

As I see it, there's only one drawback: Their bracts and flowers don't produce fragrance. But so what? I can live with no fragrance with all these other pluses.

Orchids

Description Orchids appear to be the supreme gardening achievement—the result of years of expert care given by an accomplished gardener; but many of these plants (a small number of the thousands of known types) are grown effortlessly by beginners. Beginners who are timid about learning orchid culture perhaps could first gain experience and confidence by mastering the culture of a number of tropicals and bromeliads. Then they can reward themselves by getting started with a few easy orchids and begin yet another level of botanical study.

If orchids have a bad name, it probably comes from the difficulty in getting them to reflower. Some need the special conditions of a drop in the night temperature, high humidity, special food, and specific temperature ranges. But there are some that will flower under windowsill conditions. Try the Peruvian clam-shell orchid *(Epidendrum cochleatum)* in an east-facing window and grow it in fir bark chips. Moth orchid *(Phalaenopsis)* hybrids are good for beginners, too. Use coarse fir bark chips to pot them in. This one is easy to reflower.

A blooming orchid is exquisite, but when the plant isn't in bloom, it's ugly. This is where bromeliads differ from orchids. You don't have to set a bromeliad back out of sight so that it won't attract attention by its ugliness, but many orchid growers do this when their orchids aren't blooming.

Orchids are able to take moisture and nourishment from the air. They store water in bulblike structures called "pseudo-bulbs," though not all orchids have them. Some orchids are terrestrial. They don't live above the ground—they live on the ground with their roots in the loose soil; they aren't able to hold water very well because they don't have pseudo-bulbs.

Culture Generally speaking, orchids require about the same humidity, air circulation, and warm temperatures as bromeliads (above 55°F in the winter). Many need bright light for 10 to 15 hours a day, but no direct sun. Naturally, you'll want to check each plant's light needs, just to be on the safe side. They also do well under artificial lights. Consult plant directories or individual plant tags for water requirements, because some prefer to dry out briefly between waterings, yet others like a more moist medium.

It may surprise you to know that orchids have a worldwide habitation, which includes even frigid regions. Some live high in the mountains (in the Andes, for example), and gardeners wishing to cultivate them need special cooling equipment to drop the temp to a desirable range. We aren't talking about delicate plants here. Orchids are tough, durable, and tolerant. Just look at the way they grow and where they grow, and you easily can see that they have no difficulty adapting.

As far as potting medium goes, tree fern fiber (which holds water well) has been used, and it stays intact for ages, allowing air to get to the roots. Some gardeners say they have great success by mixing coarse perlite with it. Fir bark chips decompose after a while, and this means more repotting for you. I used to use osmunda fiber, because the old orchid books highly recommended it, and I was able to buy it; but I don't see it anymore.

Orchids have a dormancy cycle just like tropicals, cacti, and other plants. This occurs for most of the autumn and early winter. It's during this time that they're so ugly. Some of them lose all of their leaves and become only bare pseudo-bulbs. It's best to put dormant orchids out of sight in your collection, and allow the tropicals to camouflage them with their foliage.

There isn't much to do when orchids are dormant (as with any plant that's dormant). They just sit there. Pseudo-bulb orchids don't need a lot of water because they can store it. Other orchids may need occasional water, but on the whole, water needs lessen during dormancy. The potting mix shouldn't be allowed to dry out completely, however. When growth finally picks up again, put the plants back in their front-row seat and begin watering and feeding as usual. And, as always, don't use cold water on them.

I collect rainwater for all my orchids and bromeliads and store it in drums. But you may not be able to accommodate a setup like this if you're an apartment dweller or if you live in the city. In this case, leave your plants indoors. If you have decent rainwater, you can summer orchids outdoors in light shade and let them catch all the rain they want. After fetching and carrying for all my plants during the winter, I'm more than willing to let Mother Nature tend them in the spring and summer.

But what do you do when you go away for summer vacation? Drop the indoor temperature and water all the orchids thoroughly before you leave, and you'll get a week away without problems. If you'll be gone longer, use a capillary mat (see p. 129). If your plants are in the greenhouse, use shade cloth and don't forget to keep the air circulating. You could ask another orchid grower to drop in and look at your plants during the second week of your absence (well-watered plants should be fine during the first week you're gone).

Types of orchids to try Some orchids you might want to try are the cattleyas, phalaenopsis, paphiopedilums, intermediate miltonias, brassavolas, and epidendrums. Mail-order catalogs will steer you in the proper direction.

This is a good time to put in a favorable word for the orchid societies in your area. Their help is immeasurable, because their ranks comprise all ranges of expertise. If you develop a real interest in this plant, you may want to join an orchid club or society. Local clubs have orchid shows and sell plants at lawn and garden shows. These shows are excellent times to take a member aside and ask questions. They'll also have literature and handouts available to you—usually for free. Club members often trade divisions with one another, and this is an excellent way to get an expensive plant. If you want to join a national club, there's always the American Orchid Society, which may have a chapter in your area.

Tips If you notice that your orchids have scale, spider mites, mealybugs, or other insect pests, you can dip them.

Commercial insecticidal soaps are mild and can usually do the job. Simply follow the manufacturer's instructions: Fill a bucket with warm water, add the recommended amount of soap, hold on to the plant and soil mix, turn the pot over, and plunge it into the solution. Swirl the foliage around in the bucket.

Don't forget to stake flowering plants that need it. I use green-colored cane sticks (you've seen them in garden centers) to stake my orchids because they look more natural and won't take attention away from the beauty of the flowers. For long spikes in bloom, I insert a long cane at an angle and tie the spike with green-colored twist ties—some people like to use string. I don't because I need an extra pair of hands, and the spike often outlasts the string, causing me more rework time. If you locate an orchid club in your area, members can give you addresses for catalogs so that you can purchase the clips and wire stakes that your needs require.

I've seen many more orchids on the market lately. This is because of modern propagation techniques that cut down on the production time of new plants.

Before you know it, grocery stores will start carrying them just as they do African violets and bromeliads. You'll be able to buy a flowering-size cattleya orchid for a reasonable price. The prices also have dropped to the point that almost anyone can buy them. When you do buy, select an older plant (if possible), because it takes years for young plants to reach blooming age. You also could get a cattleya orchid in sheath (the flower buds are about ready to open) just to satisfy your curiosity and to see if the plants are something you'd like to cultivate.

When some gardeners master a particular plant culture, they take up another as a new challenge. If this sounds like you, I suggest that you begin with some inexpensive orchids, because, as always, when learning new plant culture, you're starting at the bottom all over again. You vacate your well-deserved expert status and return to student status. You must prepare yourself once again to be willing to lose a few plants in order to gain experience. If you can't, you won't learn. You can't become an expert on orchid culture by reading a book—you must put

your hands on them. Once you have the culture under your belt, purchase a few of the more expensive ones. You will have earned them.

Moth Orchid (Phalaenopsis *species*)

Description This plant's common name reflects the blooms' appearance— they look like a cluster of large moths. Dozens of blooms float along tall stems that reach 2 ft. to 4 ft. in length. When you see moth orchids, other orchids will seem gaudy by comparison to their simple beauty.

Moth orchids are perhaps the best orchids for beginners and are among the most beautiful of all orchids when in flower. Beginners will be delighted to know that they're also the most free-flowering orchids there are, blooming mostly in the winter.

Their coloring ranges from white (used in bridal bouquets) to yellow, pink, and pink-striped. Plants can grow to 30 in. tall, and flower sizes range from 2 in. to 5 in.—impressive. Depending on the kind of phalaenopsises you have, you'll be able to enjoy those blooms anywhere from 21 to 100 days.

The first flowers to open on the moth orchid will be those on the lower part of the stem. Each bud opens in succession toward the tip of the stem. Soon, all blooms are open, and the sight is magnificent. In fact, the stem will be so heavy that you'll need to stake it.

As this orchid grows, the bottom leaves eventually will turn yellow. Don't be alarmed—it's normal. Since they won't pull off easily, just clip them off with scissors, and the plant won't look so unsightly.

Moth orchids hold their exotic blooms for weeks. (Photo by Erik Simmons.)

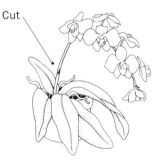

Cutting back a moth orchid

Cut

After a moth orchid has finished blooming, cut the stem back to the first node below the flower stem to encourage another flower stem to grow.

Culture

- **Light.** Moth orchids like shade in the summer with brighter light the rest of the year—no direct sun.
- **Water.** Keep the medium barely moist at all times, but be careful not to overwater. If possible, use rainwater, and don't use cold water.
- **Temperature.** Keep daytime temperatures at 75°F and nighttime temperatures at 65°F.
- **Humidity.** Same as tropicals: 50%. Moth orchids are well suited to home humidity, but they must have excellent air circulation. Use your ceiling fan.
- **Potting.** Phalaenopsises lack pseudobulbs and can be repotted any time of the year, but it's best to wait until the plant has finished flowering—so repot in the spring. When you see them trying to climb out of their pots, displaying lots of roots, it's time to shift up. In fact, you'll probably be repotting every two years. Moth orchids grow vertically (they're monopodial) and can be set in the pot without the specific positioning that cattleya orchids need.

  This orchid mix is a favorite of some growers: 2 parts fir bark and 1 part coarse peat moss with a little slow-release fertilizer mixed in.
- **Feeding.** Feed after they come out of dormancy.

Tip When your moth orchid flowers fade, cut the stem at the first bract *below* the flower cluster. You'll get another stem of flowers (possibly two) from the cut stem. This is yet another reason to grow them—they always seem to be blooming.

Herbs for Your Garden Room

In the past, few people planted herb gardens purely for enjoyment; early herb gardens were for medicinal and culinary use. But in the 1990s, pleasure herb gardens really took off. Now almost everyone grows some kind of herb, whether it's for cooking or not. People just like the way herbs smell. The interest in them has skyrocketed. Of all the lectures I've given over the past five years, the ones on herb gardening have been in most demand.

But why should herb gardeners be the only people to have a supply of herbs? There are many herbs that'll grow well on a sunny windowsill or in a plant room. Of course, if you have a greenhouse, your prospects are even better for a good crop. If you already have an herb garden, I suggest that you pot up a few of your favorite culinary herbs and bring them indoors so that you'll have them close at hand for use in the kitchen during the winter months. If you grow herbs only for their foliage and aromatic oils, not only will you be able to enjoy their scent in the plant room, but you'll also be pest-proofing your other plants. Herbs do tend to deter insect pests.

But herbs can be used in other ways. Try them in potpourris, soaps, bath splashes, moth bags, sachet pouches, and insect and rodent repellents. One word of warning: If you intend to use your herbs for cooking, *never* use toxic insecticides on them.

Rosemary (Rosmarinus officinalis)

Description Rosemary is an herb that grows in the sunny Mediterranean region where the climate offers little rain and hot temperatures in the summer. If you see it growing in an outdoor herb garden, it appears as a shrub. And it can become a large plant if its requirements are met. I've seen it grow anywhere from a few feet to 6 ft. tall, and in a greenhouse, it should reach from 2 ft. to 4½ ft.

Herbs, which can be used for topiary, can provide beauty for the eye and flavor for your meals. (Photo by Derek Fell.)

Its delicate, tiny leaves are gray-green and redolent with volatile oils, which adhere to the skin even if your hand simply brushes against the foliage. Small lavender, blue, or pink flowers appear in the spring and sometimes in the fall. But if your light exposure is good, the plant also will flower for you in the winter.

This sweetly scented herb is an excellent subject for topiary. I keep these little trees indoors during the winter to scent the plant room, but once the last frost of spring is over, I put them out to spend the summer on the stone wall so they can sun themselves with the thyme and lavender.

Rosemary is hardy in Zones 7 to 10, so bring it back indoors with your other houseplants for the fall. Greenhouse gardeners will like rosemary because it repels moths.

Culture

- **Light.** Rosemary prefers full sun outdoors, so a window position in a south- or west-facing window suits it well.
- **Water.** The soil must dry a little between waterings, but don't let the plant go bone dry for long periods. If it wilts, it doesn't recover. Certain parts of the plant may die and will have to be cut out. This is bad news if your plant has been trained into a topiary form, because new growth will have to be encouraged from the gaping hole left in the foliage. I experienced this problem a few years ago during an exceptionally hot summer. One year later, the plant had filled in the hole with supple new growth—no permanent damage was done.
- **Temperature.** Rosemary likes a winter temp of 55° or 60°F.
- **Humidity.** Same as your tropicals: 50%.
- **Potting.** Use a well-drained mix with a soil base. Add a little lime to the potting mix and the oils will be even more fragrant. But don't choose a rich mix. It sounds peculiar, but if you pamper rosemary (and most other herbs) with a rich mix or fertilizer, the quality of its volatile oil decreases—it isn't as potent.
- **Harvesting.** You can snip rosemary any time for use in the kitchen. But if you're harvesting bunches of it from large pot plants in your greenhouse, cut your stems when the flowers are in bud.

  As with most herbs you use in cooking, keep all flowers pinched off. Flower production lessens the potency of the volatile oils in the leaves.
- **Preserving.** You can freeze rosemary in labeled freezer bags, but when you use it in a recipe, the taste will be stronger than the fresh herb—add less of the herb than you normally would. Rosemary also can be preserved by hang drying. Gather the stems into a small bunch and tie them with a rubber band. Hang them out of the light and heat for two to three weeks or until the foliage is dry; then strip the stems of leaves. Put the leaves into labeled glass jars (don't use a metal lid—use glass tops only) for use in the kitchen. Be sure to store your herbs away from the heat and out of the sun.

Leave a few stems of rosemary hanging on your herb-drying rack for use when you barbecue in the summer. Strip the stems and toss the leaves onto the fire to flavor meats. I also like to toss the stems and leaves into the fireplace in the winter—the aroma is heavenly. Use your rosemary in pork, chicken, fish, egg, and cheese dishes.

This rosemary topiary eventually will have a classic globe top.

INDEX

Page references in *italic* indicate illustrations.

A

Aeschynanthus pulcher. See Lipstick plant

African violets (*Saintpaulia ionantha*), 7, 11, *11*, 12, 18, 22, *28*, 32, 34, 69, 77, 82, *100*, 101, 111

Agapanthus africanus. See Lily of the Nile

Agavaceae. See Cordylines

Ageratums (*Ageratum*), 80

Aglaonema modestum. See Chinese evergreen

All-Purpose Insect Spray, recipe, 84–85

Aloe (*Aloe vera*), *49*

Aluminum plant (*Pilea cadierei*), 7, 11, 47

Amaryllises (*Hippeastrum*), 7, 64, 98, 101, *102*, 116–17, 120, 136–38, *136*

Anthurium scherzeranum/andreanum. See Flamingo flower

Aphelandra squarrosa. See Zebra plant

Aphids, 76, *76*, 85, *86*, 87

Arrowhead vine (*Syngonium podophyllum*), 14, *97*

Artificial light

    fluorescent tubes, buying, 12–13

    fluorescent tubes, changing, 14

    incandescent bulbs, problems with, 12–13

    list of plants for, 11

    placement of plants under, 12, *12*, 13

    watering plants under, 10–11

Aspidistra elatior. See Cast-iron plant

Asplensim nidus. See Bird's nest fern

Azaleas (*Rhododendron*), 7, 34, 77, 80, 110, *110*

B

Baby's tears (*Soleirolia soleirolii*), 47

Bamboo palm (*Chamaedorea erumpens*), 64

Basil (*Ocimum*), 80

Bathtub wicking, 129–30, *130*

Bay/sweet bay (*Laurus nobilis*), 48

Beaucarnea recurvata. See Ponytail plant

Begonias (*Begonia*), 11, 22, 32

    angel-wing (*B. coccinea*), 64

    rex (*B. × rex-cultorum*), 47

Bird-of-paradise (*Strelitzia reginae*), 32, 64

Bird's nest fern (*Asplensim nidus*), 7, 14, *14*, 47, 64, 79

Bleeding heart (*Clerodendrum thomsoniae*), 32, 106

Boston fern (*Nephrolepis exaltata* 'Bostoniensis'), 47, 64

Bougainvillea glabra. See Paper flower

Brake fern (*Pteris*), 64

Bromeliads, 7, 11, 32, 34, 36, 50, 53–54, *53*, 111, 133, 143–44, *143*, *144*

Brugmansia, 111

Butterfly flower (*Schizanthus*), 48

C

Cacti, 7, 26–27, *28*, 34, 48, 50, 77, 82, 133

Calamondin orange (*Citrofortunella mitis*), 32, 48

Cape jasmine (*Gardenia jasminoides*), 32

Cape primrose (*Streptocarpus × hybridus*), 32

Capillary mats, 129, *129*

Capsicum annuum. See Ornamental pepper

Cast-iron plant (*Aspidistra elatior*), 7, 14, 50, 64, *64*, 111

Castor-oil plant (*Ricinus communis*), 14, 48

Cellular collapse, 15, *15*

Chain stores, buying plants from, 92

Charcoal, *35*, 36, *36*, 73

Chenille plant (*Acalypha hispida*), 32

Chinese evergreen (*Aglaonema modestum*), 7, 14, *14*, 64, 111

Chlorophytum comosum. See Spider plant

Chlorosis, 53, 54

Christmas cactus (*Epiphyllum* and Schlumbergera bridgesii), 26, *26*, 97, 120

Chrysanthemums (*Chrysanthemum*), 7, 80

Cigar plant (*Cuphea ignea*), 32

Citrofortunella mitis. See Calamondin orange

Citrus (*Citrus*), 7, 77, 79

Clematis, 'Sweet Autumn' (*Clematis paniculata*), 103

Clerodendrum thomsoniae. See Bleeding heart; Glory-bower

Clivias (*Clivia miniata*), 7, 61, 62, 64, 120, 121–22, *122*, 135

Clog plant (*Nematanthus glabra*), 32

Clubs, plant, 88–89

Cold weather

    plants sensitive to, 32

    moving plants during, 32

Coleuses, 7, 111

Columnea × banksii/C. gloriosa. See Goldfish plant

Constant-feed method, 52–53

Cordylines (*Agavaceae*), 7, 14

Cordyline terminalis. See Ti plant

Corn plant/palm (*Dracaena fragrans* 'Massangeana'), 5, 47

Crown-of-thorns (*Euphorbia milii splendens*), 32, 62

Crown rot, 81–82, *82*

Cultural requirements, 4–5

Culture tags. *See* Plant tags

Cyclamens (*Cyclamen persicum*), 7, 11, 18, 22, 76

    florist's, 47

D

Daisies, gerbera, 80

Delta maidenhair (*Adiantum raddianum*), 47

Dieffenbachia (*Dieffenbachia*), 7, 111

Diseases

    remedies, 82–87, *84*

    See also specific types

Dormancy cycle, 113

Double-potting, 21–22, *21*, 28, 45, 109

PUBLISHER: Suzanne La Rosa
ASSOCIATE PUBLISHER: Helen Albert
EDITORIAL ASSISTANT: Cherilyn DeVries

EDITOR: Candace B. Levy
PROJECT MANAGER: Linda Glick Conway
DESIGNER/LAYOUT ARTIST: Jonathon Nix
ILLUSTRATOR: Robin Brickman
PHOTOGRAPHER (except where noted): Scott Phillips

TYPEFACES: Minion and Franklin Gothic
PAPER: 70 lb. Lithoweb Dull
PRINTER: RR Donnelley & Sons Company